FINDING YOUR FEET

Corinne Hutton

FINDING YOUR FEET
PUBLICATIONS

Published in 2017 by Finding Your Feet Publications

Copyright © Corinne Hutton 2017

ISBN Paperback: 978-1-9997116-0-3
Ebook: 978-1-9997116-1-0

A CIP catalogue copy of this book can be found
in the British Library.

Front cover photograph courtesy of John Linton Photographers.
Back cover photograph courtesy of Simon Murphy.

Published with the help of Indie Authors World

IndieAuthors
World

DEDICATION

I never, ever forget how much my amazing group of friends and family did for me during my trauma, in my rehabilitation, and still do for me now.

I totally credit them and my fabulous son, Rory, when I reflect on how far I've come and how well I manage, in my positivity and determination to REALLY live.

It's always as a result of their love, their bullying, and their friendship, and my will to be a good role model and 'hands on' mum.

I can't say 'thank you' often enough.

TWINKLE, TWINKLE, LITTLE STAR

DO YOU KNOW HOW LOVED YOU ARE?

I do!

ACKNOWLEDGEMENTS

Thanks to Tom Lucas for encouraging me to write the book and for volunteering the wonderful editor Christine McPherson who spent months and months encouraging me to start writing even a chapter, then pushing me until I had finished it. She then altered it as I changed my mind several times or remembered a missing story. Thank you for being so patient Christine, for no reward or payment. You have been wonderful.

Publishers, Indie Authors World, also had their work cut out with my inexperience, my opinionated posse and our vision for the book. Sorry and thanks Kim & Sinclair. I hope we've collaborated well.

FOREWORD

The courage and resolve Corinne has shown impressed me greatly when we met, and I was particularly struck by her determination to make things better for other people.

Corinne's experience and attitude is truly inspiring and I am sure that this book will be of great support to others. Corinne, from the moment one meets her, has a natural aptitude to make a person feel at ease with what happened to her.

NICOLA STURGEON

First Minister of Scotland

*

With Corinne there exist no taboos; "It is what it is" — a phrase she used on our first meeting that stayed with me. Because Corinne somehow manages to accept the fate that befell her. Indeed, she uses her own misfortune to exact positivity, impetus, and motivation on the lives of others.

Corinne has not let her amputations prevent her achieving whatever she wants to achieve — from breaking world records and climbing mountains to being a wonderful mum to Rory.

Wherever Corinne's life was headed before she lost her limbs, it begs the question as to whether her life would be quite so extraordinary had this twist of fate not happened. The public, the media, the sports community, and the medical profession follow her progress and her undeniable influence with increasing interest and adoration.

Having lived and breathed the world of sport from the age of 16, I've had the honour of meeting some of the greatest players and managers to grace the world of football — individuals with whom I see in Corinne the same spark, determination, and grit so rarely found.

Perhaps if all those in the world of sport could adopt an attitude akin to that of Corinne, sport would be in an even better place.

MICHAEL O'NEILL

*Northern Ireland National Football Team Manager
and Finding Your Feet Ambassador*

*

Corinne is an extraordinary woman who has turned sheer bad luck into something positive and she is a force for good in our part of the world. I can only look and admire and wonder how many people would have been that brave. She made me look at my own soul and I was found wanting by comparison

JOHN BEATTIE

*Scotland International & British Lions Rugby Star,
now BBC presenter and Finding Your Feet Ambassador*

CONTENTS

PROLOGUE

Why did I write this book?

Actually, because a few people said I should — and I always do as I'm told! Seriously, I just felt it would be a good way to ensure that I never forget the horror of what I went though and to remind myself of how far I have come.

Maybe I wrote it for Rory. He'll never remember or comprehend what happened, what might have been, and how much he influenced my fightback unless he reads this.

Maybe I wrote it, too, for the countless people to whom I owe so much. To say 'thank you' won't ever be enough, but to give credit here might make them feel appreciated. In fact, some agreed to contribute and have done so in their own style – some witty, some clever and some emotional additions that I hope make the book more enjoyable.

Most of all, I think I want to give some hope to people who have faced a life-changing trauma and who need to find their feet. If my story, or my learning curve, helps to make a small difference to one person, or inspires another to keep fighting, then the arduous task of typing with no fingers has been worthwhile. I can't repeat often enough, 'Yes you can — if you want to enough.'

Sometimes positive things are born from tragic events, and certainly more doors open with opportunity now than they ever did for me before. At one point I asked myself if my life had been worth saving. No hands, no legs, no prospects. Well, let me tell you how silly I feel now for thinking that.

I'm about to tell you why.

DAVY, BIG BROTHER -
TWENTY FOUR HOURS

'Corinne in hospital with pneumonia, under control,' the text message said. I was in the sunshine in the parade at the village gala day... June 8th, 2013.

As I reach the hospital, my mum sits alone in the hospital room. She is in tears and is exhausted. She has just driven with my dad from Devon, where they'd been on holiday. I take one look at my sister connected to an assortment of machines and I know instantly it's bad.

Having persuaded my parents that it's all under control, I manage to get them to go home and get some rest. I can see the relief in my mum's eyes: 'Davy says it's ok.' The pit of my stomach was telling me it wasn't.

I set about finding out what all the machines were doing... I learn quickly.

Temperature's at 42; I know inside she's literally cooking. In desperation, they transfuse frozen blood into her to cool her... no one knows what's causing it. 'You know she's very *sick, Davy, don't you?' 'Of course I know she's fucking sick. Make her not sick!' I'm shouting, demanding, pleading. I can see the life leaving her hands and feet, travelling up her limbs in a kind of death march. Suddenly her temperature drops; it's the first sign of hope.*

It's 1am. I phone my brother in Dubai. 'Do I need to get on a plane, Davy?' he asks. My forehead is against the corridor wall. 'Yes, Scobe, you do.' I hate myself for saying it out loud.

Within two hours my brother is on the Emirates flight to Glasgow. Emirates are a very helpful airline. He texts to say he's on the plane, just as Doctor Brian tells me her temperature has started to rocket. She's trying to die; we still don't know why. I'm glad my brother doesn't know this bit.

'Can you keep her alive until he gets here?' I ask Brian. I train in the gym with him… he knows Cor. Nurses and doctors are visibly upset, no one has gone home, more have come in, everyone is included in the brainstorming, including me. Think, ffs! Within the hour, the hospital phone my parents and tell them they should come in immediately.

They go to collect Russell — Corinne's husband. I think they still don't understand the situation. They would within the hour, and it's horrible to watch the reality grab them. As my folks arrive, I'm a wee boy again. I remember crying, 'I can't save her, Mum.' It was the first time I wasn't in control of myself since I was a child. I'm in bits. I see my mum's eyes and get a grip of myself. We have a four-year-old boy to look after now… focus.

Kate dumps Huckleberry with Pete and Tam; he has a *karate exam that morning (Huck, not Pete. Pete's rubbish at karate). I phone Emma in Dubai, Janie and Elaine… I speak to Maggie in Texas, Lynne in Seattle, George in Ireland. Everyone heads for an aeroplane; we're a tight crowd that way. My phone starts to ring constantly. Scott, Nigel in Dublin, Ally Common in Dubai, 'What the fuck Davy?!' To a man, they say the same things, genuine and distraught. I take all the calls and I'm glad of them all. It's like knowing everyone is in the room with me; I have great friends. I phone Mo. This one is difficult. Fabio answers, I can hear Mo; she knows why I'm calling. 'NOOOOO… NOOOOO!' She refuses to take the handset. Her noises are horrible, like a wounded animal, an unnatural howl. She has to say goodbye.*

I have to go and get her. It takes me 15 minutes to get there. Karen is there, Alan comes in. Alan is a medical man; he's been in contact all night with me and the doctors. Everyone was involved in the brainstorm.

I drive back, prepare wee Mo for what she will see. We enter the room. Kate is stroking Cor's arm and, as usual, is in command; she's very capable. Pauline, the doctor, looks at me. She has tears running down her cheeks… 'There's a unit in Leicester, Davy, they're sending a plane for her. They're on their way.'

In a fraction of a second, I experience disbelief, euphoria, panic… my knees give out. Will she survive the flight, the procedure? My brother arrives. 'Take us to Leicester, someone. There's some fight left in my sister.'

Huck passes his karate exam, and we pass the 24hr mark.

CHAPTER 1
LIFE BEFORE

I used to think I was wealthy. I had a good job, nice car, a nice house, and exciting holidays. I was no angel, but I ate reasonably well, exercised regularly, and didn't smoke or drink to excess. I challenged myself — a lot — for good charitable causes, and I tried to be caring and supportive to my family and be a good mum and friend. My life was good, but I didn't really, honestly 'make a difference'. Yet, I would probably have lived like that, happily, forever.

I look back now and realise I'd suffered a few knocks in recent years. My family's 35-year-old business failed and I took responsibility for that, later finding out that they felt guilty, too. They'd all retired or moved on to other careers and left me with this sinking ship, they felt. I'd had two miscarriages before I decided I was lucky with my healthy, happy, wee Rory — some people don't get even that! I was the victim of some devious business theft and let down by people I trusted and had helped, but thought 'what goes around comes around'. And I lost a close friend to cancer.

I didn't ever think I was stressed, but I guess I had stresses in my life. Enough knocks for my system to be low, perhaps?

One Friday in June 2013, after suffering a bad cough for two weeks and sharing germs with my colleagues, I'd had enough. It was just a cough and you wouldn't normally panic over 'just a cough', would you? As a busy mum of four-year-old Rory, with a house to keep and a stressful job, I hadn't allowed a cough to floor me but I was spreading germs and it needed an anti-biotic. After a thorough check, the doctor seemed to agree with me and I came home, took the drugs, and went to bed. It was to be a glorious summer weekend for the village fete, and I wanted to feel better.

But the next morning I was worse. I was sick all over my bedroom floor (wooden, fortunately) and there was a lot of blood in it. As that happened, Rory came running in and I had to chase him back downstairs so he didn't see too much. Even then, I thought it must be a bug or virus, as you do. With a bit of persuasion, I agreed to call NHS 24 to ask for advice, as the doctor's surgery is closed on a Saturday. They sounded uncon-cerned, too, but suggested I go up to see them, to be safe. The journey was hot, and I was feverish and felt a bit faint, but I got there… just.

I wasn't left to wait at all. I must have looked bad! I was taken straight in to a doctor who immediately asked me to move to a bed. I must have looked *really* bad! I collapsed before reaching it. The last thing I remember is medics all around me.

Dr. Brian Lafferty, MBChB - The Medic

One summer night a few years ago, I started a shift that I would remember for a long time. I was working at the Royal Alexandra Hospital in Paisley, looking after the seriously ill patients in Inten-  *sive Care. Corinne had been brought into the department very sick, and had been failing every therapy we had been giving her.*

I was on nightshift when she was admitted, and looked after her on the first, very unstable night. She was in multi-organ failure, as a result of a very bad pneumonia — very unusual for someone her age. We very quickly had to support her heart and lungs, then before long her kidneys, too.

Despite our best efforts and maximising everything we had available in the hospital, Corinne continued to deteriorate and we were left with only one option. A centre in England offered a therapy called ECMO — Extracorporeal Membrane Oxygenation — a specialised piece of equipment that takes blood from your body and does the work of the heart and lungs. Ultimately, this gives the organs a chance to rest and recover, while taking over the role they can no longer manage themselves.

It was an unpleasant night to see someone so young incredibly unwell, and it was made even more personal to me because I knew Corinne's family from the local gym. I saw her father each morning before work, and her brother most evenings.

I had spent most of that night with Corinne and, when it became obvious she was going to have to be moved to the

specialist centre in England, I had to call in her parents to explain this. We are trained not to show emotion and to remain professional when explaining our actions to relatives, etc, but I found it incredibly difficult breaking this bad news to the family that morning.

I phoned each day Corinne was in England receiving ECMO therapy, to find out her progress not only for myself but for the entire department, who were keen to see her get better. We soon got word that Corinne would be returning to Paisley.

It was brilliant that Corinne had won this fight with her illness, but the war was not over, as the infection had taken its toll, involving her hands and feet. I remember most days that Corinne spent in the RAH, but none more than when young Rory, her son, came to visit for the first time; a very emotional moment.

It was a pleasure looking after Corinne, as she seemed so genuinely grateful for everything that we were doing for her. We were sad as a department when she left us to go, firstly, to a main ward, and then onto the GRI to undergo further surgery which would aid her recovery. I still get asked by colleagues how Corinne is getting on, and they are astounded when they learn of the progress she has made.

When I visited Corinne at the Glasgow Royal Infirmary, it seemed she had made more friends in the wards there, which was no surprise.

It was many months later than I next saw Corinne face-to-face. It was in the gym one afternoon when I went for a swim. Corinne was in the pool doing some lengths with her mum's supervision. I have never witnessed such determination.

It is very obvious Corinne has fantastic friends and family who have surrounded her throughout her illness, giving her much help and support. It is great seeing her back doing some exercise and, unsurprisingly, making great progress with her recovery. Patients often get held back by being negative and giving up in the face of severe illness, but it was an inspiration to witness such determination and fight from Corinne when all the medicines and machines were failing to make her better.

It is this drive and enthusiasm to get better that has saved Corinne, and I hope it remains with her in the next phase of her recovery.

***

Scott, little brother: Heading Home

OK, Corinne has pneumonia. No big deal: a friend of mine in Dubai had recently come out of hospital after suffering the same thing, and I wasn't too worried. All she needed was rest and recuperation. WRONG!

I headed to work on Sunday morning (in Dubai, our work-ing week is Sunday-Thursday) and took a call from Davy. He'd had a rough night at the hospital with Corinne, and things were not well; nor was Corinne. Never mind my rest and recuperation, Corinne was now looking straight down the barrel and it looked like I was getting on a plane to say goodbye to my big sister! This is the girl who looked after me as a kid; the girl that I wouldn't cross the road without; the girl I used to chase around the house with frogs!

Holy sh*t! Corinne was dying!

I think it was mid-morning. Within 10 minutes of getting off the phone to Davy, Emma, the kids and I were booked on the 2pm flight from Dubai to Glasgow. I called Emma and asked her to head home and get the kids from school. I drove home in a daze — I don't really remember much, to be honest. I do, however, remember being on the phone to Kate, and asking if I had to pack a suit.

We were all ready to go within half an hour, and heading to the airport. Unfortunately, it turned out that Harrison's passport was with Immigration, which meant he wasn't going anywhere. And being only a few months' old, he wasn't quite ready to stay home alone! Did it cross my mind that my kids should get home to say goodbye to their Auntie Cor? Probably, but I don't remember that. Turns out that there are a few things that I have chosen to remember and, more to the point, things I have chosen to forget. I maintain that I never, at any point, thought that Corinne was going to die, but then Emma reminds me that I phoned her and said that Corinne was dying. Again, I don't remember that.

So, Emma and the kids dropped me at the airport while I went on alone. Emma would sort out Harrison's passport, and she and the kids would join me as soon as they could. Long flight alone, then. My memory is a bit selective at this point again. I maintain that Corinne was not dying and that the really bad news came while I was in the air. I think I managed to convince myself of that, as I am sure that I did not travel thinking that. Yes, I knew she was in a fight, but I was sure she was going to win it. My brother and I are generally considered to be big guys, but Corinne is the one with all the fight!

I don't really remember the flight — it kind of passed by in a daze. I am sure I watched a movie, but I have no idea what. I think I had a couple of beers, but nothing much. I just drifted through that flight with my head not really able to focus on anything. I suppose I couldn't bring myself to think of Corinne gone, so whenever my head went there, I immediately redirected it elsewhere! I'm no psychologist but it is interesting to see your coping mechanisms when you are on board a seven-hour flight, while at some level fearing the worst.

Next thing I remember is walking through Arrivals at Glasgow Airport and there was family friend, Scott Campbell, to meet me and take me to the hospital. By this time, Scott was pretty positive as there had been a lot of developments while I was in the air. I believe that at one stage they were keeping Cor alive so I could say goodbye, and then came the 'Hail Mary' pass — the ECMO team riding in on white horses! I had no idea what ECMO was, or who the team was, but Scott quickly brought me up to speed.

I arrived at the hospital in Paisley to find the family holed up in a visitors' room. A pretty cramped visitors' room at that stage but, on the whole, a pretty positive one. It turns out that no-one was certain what this ECMO thing was all about, but the doctors had given everyone hope, and while I was arriving at the hospital they had made an initial assessment and managed to hook Corinne up to their lifesaving equipment.

The first time I saw Corinne, she was hooked up to the portable machines and the medics were all smiling — that had to be a good sign. From what everyone else tells me, this was the first bit of good news they had heard in a long time.

What did Corinne look like at that stage? Not at her best, in fairness! She had a massive machine lying on her chest and some fairly major wires connected to her. Again, I am hazy on the details — maybe I drank more than I think on the plane, or maybe I am blocking details — but Cor definitely looked better than I had been expecting.

Within half an hour of meeting the ECMO team, Cor was in an ambulance on the way to the airport for a flight to Leicester. Scott Campbell, Davy, and I followed soon after. Scott drove us all to Leicester, where we set up base camp in another visitors' room. That wasn't a comfortable night, but I think it was probably worse for Corinne!

A charity climb in the Himalayas with Dad, Arlene and Irene

Big brother Davy

Kate, Emma & Me (with limbs!)

Mum

Scott and Emma

Rory

Cheers

On The Kilt Walk

CHAPTER 2
CLOSE CALL

Acute Pneumonia, flooded lungs, together with a Streptococcal virus A (which apparently lives dormant in us all) in places it shouldn't have been, and together they caused sepsis. WHAM, BAM! My family are saying goodbye; I'm being kept alive for my young brother, Scott, to arrive on a flight from Dubai; and there is less than a 5% chance of me living.

I now know the trauma doctors who had the hard job of trying to save me, and I have heard their account of the fight we were all losing. They also had to contend with the full might of the Hutton family in 'there-must-be-a-way' battle mode, so they couldn't give up! Against their expectations, I survived the night, with my older brother, Davy, taking all the responsibility on his (thankfully broad) shoulders. He was communicating with nurses and doctors, trying to learn all the terminology and what each machine was doing, and relaying that to family and friends, whilst considering funeral options and how to help bring up his nephew, Rory, without his mum.

Fortunately, one doctor suggested they should try ECMO, and called to see if I was eligible. This rare machine — 'Extra Corporeal Membrane Oxygenation' — does the work of the lungs, in my case, and oxygenates the blood outside the body whilst chilling it to bring down body temperature. The ECMO team was in Leicester, and they agreed to fly a crew up to see me. I later learned that my stats were so poor that they weren't confident of being able to take me.

When they arrived, Scott described them as knights in shining armour with their trusty ECMO steed, and he instantly felt like there was hope. Unfortunately, my stats had slipped and I was to be rejected. The lead consultant, Chris, later told me that his team needed to return to Leicester anyway, and that I was almost certainly going to die so there was nothing to lose in taking me. Thankfully, it was his decision on weekends; he intimated that he might have had a harder job convincing his superiors on a weekday.

So I flew to Leicester by air ambulance, while my family drove the six hours to be there with me. I had already responded to the treatment by the time they arrived. As the priority was the vital organs, the doctors warned that my extremities may suffer loss of circulation, and my hands and feet had started to turn blue/black. But I was alive, and my family were happy with that for the moment.

I spent two weeks there until I was considered stable enough to return to Paisley RAH Intensive Care. That's when they brought me slowly back to consciousness.

Only then was it explained to me exactly what my family had gone through. Not me, though. I'd slept through it all! I still fill up when I think of what I put them through, unconsciously.

Amusingly, I understand that strange dreams are common on ECMO, and I had my fair share that I can recall. One was that my hospital ward was on a boat off the coast of England and I was rocking with the waves. It turns out I was on a special bed which 'waved' to avoid bed sores! In another, I was in the laundry room in the bowels of the old hospital where the nurses wearing paper caps and aprons (like in the 60s) were folding the sheets underneath me and ordering me to 'roll left, roll right'. Clearly, this was them changing my bed for me, and 'roll left, roll right' became a catchphrase between me and my ICU nurses. It was pretty odd, though, to dream about paper caps and aprons!

I now realise I could hear the noises in the ICU, but had confused their purpose. For example, I remember Davy and Scott arranging a party with the nurses in Leicester, and now realise they were flirting with them at my bedside, in a bid to stay sane. My trip back to Paisley in an ambulance will forever be remembered for the weirdest dream, where I was on a double-decker bus, lying on the luggage racks, while two very distant school friends had a very deep conversation beside me! They weren't even talking about me! How rude? But how strange a dream was that?

I was also aware of a heart rate monitor which gently clipped to my ear. Most people have it on their finger, but of course mine were too badly damaged. Every time I turned my head, the ear monitor came off and my life support machines would go into alert. Those machines gently beeping became quite a comfort after a while, as if it changed, the nurses panicked a bit.

***

Doreen, Mum

We had been on holiday in Devon, but my friend Gwyneth had discovered a lump and decided to fly home, leaving their car and four bicycles to take home. At that stage, we knew that Corinne had a bad cough and had been to the doctor the previous day.

A couple of hours into the journey, her husband, Russell, called to say he was taking her to hospital, as she was coughing up blood. Next we heard that she was being kept in hospital and was in an induced coma — news that made an already long journey feel endless.

I immediately phoned my son, David, but couldn't get him. I got Kate, my daughter-in-law, who simply said, 'On my way.' She wanted to take Rory to friends, but Russell decided to take him away.

We arrived at the hospital about 5pm, and I really expected that when we spoke to Corinne she would sit up and start crying. Instead, nothing. No sign of life at all. We sat by the bedside for a couple of hours, then my husband, Colin, decided to take the car and luggage home whilst I stayed. David came in shortly after, looked at me, and immediately feared the worst.

The young doctor looking after Corinne suggested I should go home for some sleep. I wasn't keen, but David insisted that he would drive me home and would phone if anything happened. We met Colin coming back, so we both went home and David returned to the hospital.

Sleep wasn't easy, and when I phoned at 5.30am the following morning, Dr Brian suggested that we came in right away. When we arrived, he said that she was going downhill rapidly, and he feared that she would not recover.

That day was endless. David and Kate arranged for our other son, Scott, to fly home from Dubai, and brought Corinne's best friend, Maureen, to say goodbye. When Maureen came in, she looked at Corinne, hung onto Kate, and screamed like a wounded animal. When she recovered, they both sat by the bedside massaging Corinne's hands which had started to turn blue. But it did no good.

The staff agreed they would try and keep Corinne alive until Scott got here.

My friend, Gwyneth, came in to sit with me around lunchtime, and her husband, Gerry, tried to keep everyone fed, but Corinne still lay inert, attached to life support machines.

About 3pm, Dr. Brian said that it had been suggested to send Corinne to Leicester where they had an ECMO machine (which basically puts oxygen into the body). We were in such a state that this news seemed wonderful. But he then explained that, at that stage, her charts were not

good enough for them to take her, and that her chances were slim anyway.

David, who was like a caged lion, paced the corridors, asking questions of the medical staff and trying to find out what drugs they were giving her. He said, 'They're pumping everything into her to try and improve her readings.' I said, 'Why don't you whisper to her that you need her to fight with?' The pair of them have always fought like cat and dog, since they were young children.

He looked at me with big tears in his eyes and replied, 'Mum, don't you think I've tried that?' I think that was the moment when I really took it in that I was going to lose this child, who I'm told looks so like me and even sounds like me.

Leicester finally agreed that they would fly up to see if they could do anything. When they arrived, they were not hopeful; they said at that moment she had virtually no hope, but they might give her a 4-5% chance. Where's the choice when there was nothing else? That was the moment that David fell apart; he told them to start as quickly as possible.

Corinne was taken to theatre while the rest of us howled. The next hours were interminable. When she came out of theatre, we all rushed out to the corridor. It was a terrible sight. She was strapped to a trolley, blood all over and machines everywhere; one was a mobile ECMO machine. Scott had just arrived, and that was his first sight of his big sister. By this time, it was about 9pm.

I wasn't convinced that she was strong enough for the journey and was terrified to leave her; I didn't think I would see her alive again. I didn't know that I had that many tears, but just didn't know what to do. I'm her mother; I should have been able to do something.

We weren't allowed to travel with her. So a friend, Scott Campbell, arrived to drive David and Scott to Leicester; Russell insisted he would drive himself; and Gwyneth refused to let us drive, so went straight to the airport and booked us on a 6am flight.

When we saw Corinne in Leicester, she was still alive, thank God. For the next week, we sat there from 1-8pm. David and Scott stayed most nights until about 10. I was absolutely terrified that she would wake up and find herself wired to loads of machines, unable to speak or move, in a strange place with no faces that she knew. So I was pleased that the boys stayed with her.

While they were there, they kept asking lots of questions of the hospital staff. By the end of a week, I am sure they had learned enough for a medical qualification. One day I went in and the nurse said that Corinne's bowels had moved. I was so thrilled that one organ had finally started working, that I sent out texts to everyone to say that Corinne had pooed!

The days passed very slowly. We hated to be parted from her, but felt so damned useless. After about ten days, we went in one morning and Colin was speaking to one of the nurses while I sat at the bedside. Suddenly Corinne's eyes shot open. That was the start of the improvement.

After a few more days, we were told that she was going back to Paisley. Once again I was worried that she wasn't strong enough to make that long journey in an ambulance, but she was heavily sedated. We left at the same time as the ambulance, but arrived about two hours before it. I was distraught, thinking the worst again, walking up and down

in the hospital drive and getting worse every time an ambulance drove up.

When she did arrive, she was completely unconscious again and couldn't be wakened. In fact, she was unconscious for a few days, but then gradually had longer wakening periods.

It was then that we realised how black her hands and feet were. They felt like leather, or worse, and she couldn't bend her hands or feet. At first I didn't grasp the significance of this; I was just so glad that she was alive.

David and I took pictures daily, and rubbed her hands and feet constantly. She could do nothing for herself, and the physiotherapists didn't know what to do with someone who had no movement in her extremities. She couldn't go to the toilet, turn pages in a book, or anything.

While she was in ICU, the staff were great and did everything they could for her. Nothing was too much trouble, and they let us stay with her more or less all day. This was the summer when the temperatures were in the high 70s and there was no air conditioning. Fans weren't allowed because of the danger of infection. We tried paper fans, little ones, and even waving magazines, but finally the wonderful staff used ward funds to buy her a Dyson fan.

Unfortunately, the ICU ran out of beds and one was urgently needed. So Corinne was transferred to the high dependency unit, and things got worse. I think that part of the trouble was that some staff didn't realise that she could do absolutely nothing with her black hands and feet.

One day she had a raging temperature and a nurse told us that she 'had a wee residual infection'. David went

ballistic. After all, we had spent the last three weeks with a desperately ill daughter and sister, who had been told by her doctor that she had a 'wee infection'.

Another week passed, and her hands and feet became blacker and thicker.

***

Ali, friend

Like most people, I was in total shock after hearing that Cor was seriously ill in hospital; more so after hearing that it was due to pneumonia, as I know what a killer it is. 10 years previously I had lost my father to it when he was only 54.

We had got the call on Saturday to say how ill she was, and straight away I realised the significance of the date, 8ᵗʰ of June – that was the day when my dad had been taken into the same hospital, only to die 10 days later on 18ᵗʰ June, 2003, as a result of septicaemia. Due to the 10 year anniversary the date had been on my mind.

The next morning I spoke to Kate, Cor's sister-in-law, who was taking her son to his karate class at the gym, wanting to keep everything as normal as possible for him. I agreed to meet her there. Davy and Do were there briefly to pick up a phone charger. I didn't know what to say, could only hug them. I heard septicaemia mentioned, her organs shutting down, and couldn't believe that the same thing was happening all over again. My dad didn't keep great health, I kept telling myself, but Cor, she is young and probably the fittest out of all my friends.

Thankfully, Cor was fit enough for them to try a treatment called ECMO, and they flew her down to Leicester. We knew that there was still only a slim chance that it would work; we were all praying. I kept telling myself, if she makes it past June 18th, she's going to be ok. It sounds silly but it was something to hang onto.

I often think about what would have happened if ECMO had been available to my dad, but I know that physically and more so mentally, my dad could not have gone through what Cor has. She may make it look easy, but I know it has been far from it.

She is a survivor and has astounded everyone with her determination; she is an inspiration to us all. There literally is no stopping her!

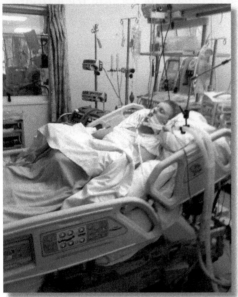

The life-saving ECMO

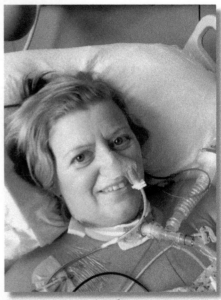

Awake

CHAPTER 3
INTENSIVE CARE

There followed three weeks of great progress. I was still on life support machines, had a tracheotomy fitted, catheters, being drip-fed, could do nothing for myself, and couldn't speak. I had frequent temperature spikes, made worse by the stunning weather and the 6 foot windows I lay beside. I take pride in knowing I was responsible for the ICU in Paisley getting their first Dyson bladeless fan, as no others were allowed for hygiene reasons!

My feet and hands were bandaged and bubble-wrapped for protection, but Davy insisted we check them every day and we knew they were getting worse. We watched as my fingers shrivelled up and went crooked, whilst the colour was now almost black. My feet were slightly better and we had great hopes for them improving, but it wasn't the priority then.

My friends had brought me photos to wake up to, and Davy's wife, Kate — my oldest bestie (she'll love that!) — had hand-drawn a keypad for me to point to if I wanted to communicate. That was both hilarious and frustrating at the same time. I actually gave up on occasions, because what I wanted to say wasn't so important anyway. My minister even visited me just to record a time when Corinne couldn't talk back!

Kate was also in charge of the visiting rota... and I believe she took it very seriously! Deciding who was allowed to visit in the earliest days, when someone became eligible to visit, how often, and for how long, were all Kate's domain... and some people broke the rules! Mum wanted all her friends to come and see me, because she was so thrilled that I was alive and wanted to show everyone. But some of my own friends hadn't yet been allowed. On a couple of occasions, a few distant friends just dropped in, and what could you do? Send them away? I was quite weak then, so I just claimed tiredness!

I had frequent unexplained panic attacks but drew inspiration from an A4 photo of Rory in his black cap and cape as he graduated from nursery. It was a day I had missed. I used him for deep breathing techniques and to remind me that there was something important to fight for. He won't have a clue how much he helped me!

An episode of rigor shakes really scared me, and that was one of very few times I had a negative nursing experience. I'd had a session with the 'tissue viability nurse' who must have one of the worst jobs ever. Poor Anne (although I think she must be a bit sadistic and have a warped sense of humour!). She scraped and cut away badly infected and decomposed skin and tissue, because it was seeping puss and gunge. It was horrific, and my stomach was churning; I think I suffered a bit of shock in having it done.

Afterwards, alone with a more mature and experienced nurse in the High Dependency Unit, I began shaking violently. All I needed was a calming word, a kind touch, and a coping mechanism. Instead she told me I had to 'deal with it' and just left me!

I tried to focus on Rory's photo to help me, but must have been visibly scared because a kind lady opposite me was so concerned that she sent her daughter over with her own little guardian angel charm. How kind! And how bad must I have been for someone in High Dependency to give away their lucky charm?

With only two exceptions (I'll explain about the other time later), I have the utmost respect and gratitude for the nurses who looked after me in my time of need. I hope they saw a fighter and a smiler, even through the worst times. That's me. I didn't want to cause trouble or make a fuss and I wanted to get better, so I really tried and really listened. Almost everyone had nothing but compassion for me, and I'll be eternally grateful to them. Every domestic, every auxiliary, every nurse, porter or doctor: you played such an important part in repairing my body and my attitude. Thank you.

One 'nice' story, and a thank you I never got the chance to say, was to a young student nurse who sat with me while a consultant drained some fluid out of my lungs. It was possibly the most painful experience I've had, and it had to be done whilst sitting up and awake so that I could help with deep or shallow breaths on demand. As the doctor inserted the huge needle in numerous places in my back to get to every separate section of my lungs, removing many syringes full of yucky fluid, the sun beat down through my 6 foot window, ensuring that the little strength I had slowly evaporated over the hour or so it took.

I was leaning on a cushion which Mor had brought me, saying 'You are my sunshine' (which was the song I had sung to Rory since he was a baby), but the hospital insisted it stay in its plastic cover for infection control reasons. Fair enough, but it wasn't helpful to my internal overheating problem! This young nurse held my hand and hugged me and cared for me when I was in real distress, cooling me with wet cloths. I won't ever forget her kindness, and I'd say she would have gone on to make a fabulous nurse.

Those three weeks since I'd returned from Leicester were almost all positive, with doctors and nurses complimenting me and congratulating me as I was taken off each machine or device, then ate for myself, breathed through my mouth, talked again, and defied all the odds — and expectations, apparently.

They called me the wonder patient, the miracle supergirl. But I'm only telling you that to emphasise the almighty crash that came after…

***

Mandy, friend and The Foot Inspector

Cor was back from Leicester but still in intensive care. Kate and Davy had kept us all up-to-date with how she was recovering. They had been worried about her hands, describing gangrene of her fingers, and now they were concerned about her feet. As I am the podiatrist in the group, they asked me if I could go in and have a look and for my opinion.

I don't specialise in this area of what we call 'high risk feet'. I work with sports people with injuries, and gait problems related to sports! The tissue viability nurses in the hospital had been looking after Cor's feet well, but the family wanted me to have a look and see what I thought about them. They just wanted to know if I could give them a prognosis of the recovery of her feet, as they were aware that the toes were looking similar to her fingers. Of course, the thought of losing fingers was bad enough, but parts of her feet as well...

This was a difficult time, as we didn't know how Corinne was going to recover. She had been so ill and was not out of the woods yet, so any straight, honest and positive news/opinions were so important to Cor and her family. I have to admit I was really looking forward to seeing her as only family had been visiting until that stage, but I was also really nervous; she is one of my closest friends, and I knew how ill she was. I have worked in healthcare for 20 years and know how upsetting it can be seeing someone you love in such a bad way.

Sitting outside intensive care waiting to be allowed in, Colin and Doreen sat opposite me, looking exhausted with the weight of the world on them. What do you say in those circumstances? It was a surreal experience. Once we were allowed in, Cor was lying on a huge bed with what seemed like a ridiculous number of machines attached to her. She recognised me and tried to smile as soon as I walked in.

Cor has always been the one in the group who is happy and positive, tries to pick you up, and makes others feel included and welcome, and today was no different. She was trying to make me feel better in that really unwelcoming environment. She tried to speak, but because she was still on a ventilator she could only mouth the words. Weirdly, I responded by whispering and mouthing my response back to her, as if it was all a big secret! I realised what I was doing and we had a bit of a laugh about it; there was nothing wrong with her hearing!

Cor's hands were bandaged up with splints on them, but I could see her fingers that were sticking out and they were black like ember. I had only ever seen gangrene once when I was a student and you never forget that look; that shocking look of dead, hard-to-the-touch tissue. And when it is on your mate, it is even more shocking!

I was there to check her feet, so I pulled the covers back to have a look and I had never seen anything like it before. They were swollen, with blistering on the top and in the arches. At first look, they didn't seem as bad as her fingers, but when checking the underside, the soles of her feet, it was obvious that the toes were headed the same way, with that blue-black colour. Her heels were also changing colour to an odd grey shade.

I realised I was way out of my comfort zone as far as foot health assessment went. I wasn't going to be able to give Cor and the family an accurate prognosis on these feet, but I knew some people who could. So I took some photos; lots of photos. I knew the family were desperate for some positive news, they'd had more than their fair share of bad news and I did not want to give any false hope or unnecessary bad news. So I tried to hide the shock I was feeling at seeing her limbs, tried to have some light conversation with Cor, and said I would ask one of my colleagues who was more skilled in this area than me.

Of course the family wanted to know that her feet were going to be saved. They had realised that there was a strong chance that she would lose her toes. They recognised the similarities between her toes and her fingers, but they were hopeful that she would lose no more than that.

My colleague later told me that there was no way to say the extent of amputation at this point, but that even if it was just the forefoot (i.e. all the toes and metatarsals) which required amputated, clinically rehabilitation is usually better with a below-knee amputation. This was not the answer the family were looking for, and they and I still hoped that her rear-foot and ankle would survive.

***

Kate, sister-in-law and great mate

No matter how much time has passed or how far she has come, it is still hard to believe the devastating events which followed so quickly in the wake of a simple cold, and changed Corinne's life forever.

I'll never forget the events of that dreadful Sunday when it looked like all hope was lost. The desperation, bewilderment, and haunted faces of her mum and dad, and brother, Davy, decisions being made to tell other family members and friends it was time to come and say goodbye, and me spending hours giving her into trouble for being lazy, just willing her to wake up and give me into trouble for being cheeky.

After Leicester decided to accept her for the ECMO treatment, all we had to do was keep her alive until they could get to Paisley. Hah! Easier said than done, as she was fighting against everything they were trying to do. With two hours still to go, one of the doctors quietly said to me that she didn't think they could keep her going that long.

Two hours, in general terms, is a nothing period of time. It passes in a blink of an eye. Anyone with children will know it's the length of time a kid's party usually lasts for. You drop them off and by the time you've got home, had a coffee, it's time to go back for them. But <u>those</u> two hours felt like weeks!

However, after a Herculean effort by the medical staff, she did make it and by the time the ECMO team had prepared her for the journey back to Leicester, her bed looked like a workbench in a busy garage! There were so many machines and tools on and around her, all you could see of her was the top of her head.

After everyone had gone off to Leicester, I was the only one left at home from the immediate family, so I suddenly found I had a new role as the 'information officer'! Ironically, I have never been so popular! My phone never stopped

ringing, as the news was getting out and so many people were calling to find out what was happening and to offer support. It was a very difficult time, repeating the story over and over again, still not knowing if she was going to make it or not. The whole situation was just surreal.

Luckily, as the saying goes, 'you can't keep a good man down!', and we were cautiously optimistic as she began passing important time markers – 24 then 48hrs passed without too much progress, but no backward steps were made, which the hospital staff told us was genuinely unexpected. They really did not think she would survive! But slowly she began to rally, and we were ecstatic when they said they thought she would make it!

After she came back to Paisley, she was still very ill and still had the tracheotomy in. That's when we discovered that we were all dreadful lip-readers! For a while it was a bit like a weird comedy routine with us answering a question like, 'what did you have for lunch?' with a reply of, 'yes, quarter past 5'! So I made up a 'word board' with lots of common words and phrases on it ranging from, 'yes; no; can I please have…; will you get me…; to F**K OFF, and I need a vodka Red Bull! Obviously it didn't work too well, but it gave her a laugh.

She was regaining her health and recovering well, but more devastation was to come.

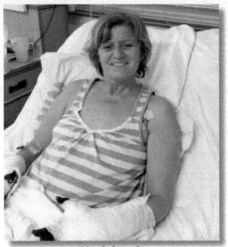

Black hands

A	B	C	D	E	F	G	H	I	J
K	L	M	N	O	P	Q	R	S	
T	U	V	W	X	Y	Z			
YES		NO		MAYBE					

Word pad 1

MUM	DAD	RORY	RUSS	KATE
DAVY	HUCK	MOR	YES	NO
CAN I HAVE….				
I DON'T WANT THAT !!				
WILL YOU GET ME….				
I NEED A VODKA REDBULL !. ☺				
F✱✱K OFF !!	😮			

Word pad 2

CHAPTER 4
LIMBITS

When I was deemed well enough (week six), I was transferred to Glasgow Royal Infirmary for what we thought would be a series of tests and scans to identify what could be saved of my hands and feet. I arrived late on the Thursday afternoon, and settled in for my first night in my new accommodation.

After breakfast, the usual 'doctor's rounds' began at 7.45 and that amounted to a visit from the consultant, several interns, the sister, a nurse, and a physio (I was getting good at identifying uniforms!).

When they reached my bedside, the consultant introduced my medical situation with these words, "Ms. Hutton is to have her legs and hands amputated later this week." He may have gone on to say more, but that's all I heard.

Stop and read that again, please, so that I make my point. "Ms. Hutton is to have her legs and hands amputated later this week."

Such crucial and tragic news delivered without empathy or humanity. Even if he thought I had known this news, those words are not to be uttered lightly in any world, not even the medical world. Somehow, I kept it together until they left the room. Just.

I was distraught and alone. I managed to dial my bedside phone to get to my parents, which was no easy task, with my black hands, brittle as charred wood. I somehow managed to relay the message as I'd been told it, and they were there, with Davy, in record time to help me.

The sister and the nurses all realised the enormity of it and really rallied for me, but I was inconsolable. I still tried to be brave, strong and positive, but all I could think of was how I would never wear flip-flops again, or walk with my son on the beach.

There followed the biggest Hutton fightback attempt in history. My family are all strong, practical, and loud, and they educate themselves when there's something they don't know. They all flew off into overdrive to prevent a quadruple amputation being the only option. I even had reiki from my good friend Brenda, who hoped she could get the energies flowing into the extremities. God love her for trying, but alas, it was to no avail. They sought second, third, and fourth opinions, hoping for a young, innovative surgeon who wanted to try something new and pioneering to save me from this fate.

Unfortunately, a pattern was emerging — and every opinion was the same, in that I had to face this horrific surgery. We had tried to get to the best surgeon suggested to us, but he was elusive. He didn't appear at a meeting arranged with my brothers, and never returned calls, leaving us (and his secretary) very frustrated and angry, along with the expected emotions of despair, helplessness, and worry.

When we gave up and booked the amputations in for the following day, lo and behold the elusive Professor Andrew Hart appeared, saying that he had cleared his diary and would be performing the surgery (along with others). I was in a huff and wanted to tell him not to bother — talk about cutting off your nose to spite your face! I suspect there was hospital politics involved, but I now consider him a friend. And I'm so grateful to him and to Dr Stephen Low for all the work they did over my six weeks of operations.

My legs were a straightforward chop-off at the calves and, apart from the infection flaring up and giving everyone in surgery a fright, it wasn't complicated. When I woke up in ICU the following day, I had a terrible experience with the ICU nurse assigned to look after me one-on-one. I'm sure I couldn't have done anything wrong whilst asleep, but she was in a wretched mood and took it out on me, which was very distressing.

I don't place myself on any pedestal, but after going through what I had, I just needed a nurse who cared about her job, not for her problems to become mine. I hope she realises now the important role she has to play.

My high dependency nurses were a dream, and a scream, and really helped me in those first weeks. God bless their wee hearts. I'm so grateful.

I had considered how my 'stumps' might look, and wasn't surprised when I first saw the result. Feet and ankles removed just below the calves. Not uncommon, I'm sad to say.

My hands were a different story, though. The surgeons removed only as much of the dead tissue and bone as they had to, and for a few days I had drains attached to remove the remaining toxic fluids. These were basically plastic bags which were sealed and attached to a pump at my feet by long tubes, and I frequently got tangled and had to be rescued!

I was left with exposed bone and tissue without any skin covering, and the best way forward — according to the surgeons — was to cut a flap in my hip and bury my hand into it, allowing the skin to attach to my remaining hand stump over time. Three weeks of time. Three weeks with my hand sewn into my hip, forming a right angle.

One nurse used to sing 'I'm a little teapot' to me, which did make me laugh. But from a practical point of view, it was a real nuisance. I couldn't move it even an inch or I might cause the circulation to fail and have to repeat the surgery. It took four nurses to turn me over on my side to clean my butt after doing the toilet. Incidentally, there is a market for someone to invent a comfortable, practical solution to doing a poo while in a hospital bed. It's near impossible to do lying flat, butt raised in an arch, with a 6" high box underneath you! I digress. Sorry.

My left arm was given a different procedure. They cut a gouge 56mm deep and 8" long from my forearm, but left it joined at the wrist. (I realise I'm mixing old school with metric, but I hope it paints the clearest picture!) They then took the gouged skin and twisted it around the remaining exposed bone of my 'hand'. This meant the circulation was continual, having never been detached from my arm. And the results are, apparently, consistently good. However, the results of both hand surgeries were horrific to look at. My left was like a snake's head dancing out of a basket in response to some snake charmer playing a flute!

Totally covered in clotted, bloody stitches from my elbow to my one remaining metacarpal (I'm learning!), it was really ugly. But both Professor Hart and Dr Stephen Low were delighted with their work, and I think they thought I was ungrateful when I saw it at first. I was disgusted and very upset.

My right hand had a nice smooth 'mitt' of skin now and looked better, but only compared to my left. However, I now appreciate what they did for me, in saving my wrists and patching me up in such a way that allowed for a better chance of more function, going forward.

One day I was transferred by ambulance to the Southern General Hospital for a consultation with a prosthetics expert. I got into an ambulance with other people and felt really self-conscious with my black legs and hands. Weeks later I met the same lady at physio, and Nan turned out to be such a big character and so much fun in rehab. I later met the ambulance staff, too; I guess I must have been quite memorable to them.

It was hugely positive for me to be told by the lovely consultant that he would fight for bionic hands for me, but I was horrified at what they showed me as being the 'realistic' legs they could give me. They wouldn't fool anyone!

When my appointment was over, I was told I may have a long wait for an ambulance. Instead, Davy took me and my wheelchair out to his big Jeep and lifted me (and my catheter bag, now called my gold Gucci bag!) into the front seat and drove me a wee detour via my work. Despite the bandaged hands and legs (and the bag!), it felt normal and it was a big deal for a lot of people who care about me to see me and know that I was okay.

Rory and my nephew, Huck, had been coming to see me weekly at that stage, and it was an operation in itself to get me prepared for those visits. Getting me into a chair involved a small crane, and my hospital 'goonie' gagged open underneath whilst I was being hoisted, and a draught could be felt. That took masses of energy and then sitting up was tiring, too, believe it or not. I could last only an hour without needing to get back to a horizontal position. My 'hands and feet' and later 'stumps' had to be covered and tubes hidden, where possible.

Huck helped Rory, as he's older and far more factual and open, so he would just ask whatever he wanted to know. One time he told me that he understood that what had happened to me was like a snake bite, and all they had to find was the antidote. The blood poisoning I had contracted wasn't too far removed from his diagnosis!

When he asked me how they would cut off my 'broken' hands and feet, I confessed that I had thought about it but that I didn't think I'd like the answer!

I was cheered up by the steady stream of friends coming to see me and make me laugh. One time I nearly cracked up when my friends Arlene and Irene (or Fran and Anna, as we like to call them) came to see me. Whilst giving me a hug as they arrived, Arlene caught her foot on my catheter pipe and seconds later, there was a pool of pee all over my room! My, how I laughed, though; and still do to this day! Laughter is definitely the best medicine.

Another day, I was allowed to go for a coffee outside the hospital. I was transferred into a wheelchair, and off I went with family. I was heavily bandaged and must have been quite a sight to strangers, but Rory wouldn't let anyone else push me. Only five years old and pushing with all his might, with his body at a 45 degree angle, he was so caring and protective, it made me burst with pride along with fighting huge feelings of guilt for what I was putting him through.

I struggled a lot with iron levels for a bit and the 'vegetables' and 'red meat' the hospital served me weren't going to help. They were served by the nicest, most helpful staff, though. At first, they even had to sit and feed me when I couldn't do it myself. I had frequent 'carryins' from nearby restaurant Celino's, who make the best steak sandwich ever, and I managed to get my levels high enough to cope with the next op. The decadence of it!

While in hospital, I was presented with a cheque from a guy at my gym, who told my brother I would need a lot of expensive things for a very long time and that he wanted to help. A few people began arranging fundraisers, but I also found that quite hard to take; embarrassing even. For someone so independent and capable, and having raised lots of money myself for lots of charities and done lots of cool challenges, I was now needy and I was the charity.

Bobby was the first of my friends to arrange a fundraiser for me, in the pub I used to own. 'Friends of Corinne'! - wishing me well and wanting to help and it was a great night but I was struggling with the effort of the brave face and with the sympathy.

We considered this as a family and saw an opportunity, first, to help me have a future; and second, to help others who have suffered similar traumas but didn't have the support I had to rebuild their lives. I could live with the charity that way, knowing I was to pay it back when I had made a recovery.

One day my brother, Scott, and my nephew, Cooper, took me to a local McDonalds for a treat (?!). As we tried to work out where I should go with my wheelchair, two ladies offered to give me their table. I replied, 'That's kind, thank you, but we're just finding our feet.' Scott started to laugh and said, 'You can't say that. You don't have any feet!'

I wonder if these ladies have a clue what they started, as that became the name of my charity.

***

The centre of a lot of discussions was the up-and-coming occasion of Rory starting primary school for the first time. How could I possibly miss that? Obviously my operations and recovery were crucial, but that was an event that could never be repeated.

As the date got closer, we plotted and planned how I could be there for Rory, and fortunately we were able to slot it in between surgeries. Dad arrived at 7am to get me and my wheelchair into the car, but that involved me being up at 5.30am to allow the nurses time to wash and dress me before their breakfast and change of shift duties!

It was a great day in my life, and the day that my son started seeing me as a normal mum again. No more cotton wool treatment or pedestals for me... and I loved it! I think there were a few damp eyes that day, as I knew a lot of people in my village of 40 years, and Scott and Emma had come specially from Dubai. Thank you, nurses, for making that happen for me.

I estimate I had over 400 nurses during my hospitalisation, and all but two were absolute angels and I'll never forget what they did for me. The one that drew happy faces on my stomach and sang the teapot song to me, gets a special mention, but I won't name her in case she gets into bother. She made me laugh, though, and that helped me so much.

Another brought me in a very thoughtful gift of a box of tokens, each meaning something kind, helpful, and hopeful for me, like a plaster to heal, and a star to wish upon. There are dozens of stories of kindness from the nurses, and I've been back to thank them a few times. There are a few I didn't manage to see again, but I hope word gets to them that they saved me and I'll make them proud.

One of my worst memories of hospital is from a night when I decided I needed the nurse for something. I can't even remember what it was, but I was a nice patient so I must have really needed something. I had a problem where I couldn't easily reach for the buzzer, so they always looped it over a bed rail to lie beside me. But this particular night, it fell down. I tried to pull the cable (with bandage boxing gloves on), but the more I tried, the further away I pushed it. I have this image of me on all fours, weak and exhausted, trying to reach over the end of the bed and failing miserably to get to it.

I was so frustrated and tried to shout to the nurses, but it was probably 10pm at that time and it was lights out. I didn't want to wake anyone, and no-one was walking past my room. I tried for maybe 20 minutes, working myself up into a panic, and I sobbed so hard for ages. I felt utterly helpless, useless, disabled, and alone. A neighbouring patient eventually heard my calls and pressed her buzzer, but by then I was a mess and inconsolable. Such a small thing we all take for granted, and it crushed me.

One day, the physios suggested that they might be able to get me upright and standing on early-stage artificial legs. My wounds were still quite raw and wouldn't take any impact or weight, but I was taken down to the hospital gym to try 'Palm aids'. These were inflatable tubes, a bit like long armbands supported in metal cages. My leg stumps were put inside the deflated tubes, inside the cages, and then the two physiotherapists inflated them to a very precise pressure. The inflated tubes padded my wounds to protect them from my body weight (although I was pretty skinny at that time), and the cages outwith were attached to poles, each sporting a rubber 'foot'.

All I would ever manage on them was to get vertical, but with a physio under each armpit, I was able to take steps forward. And by the end of the session, Mum had found me and was gobsmacked to see me walk across the gym towards her (albeit held up by my human crutches!). What a superb feeling, even if it did wipe me out trying!

***

Whilst in the final stages of my hospitalisation, I received a dreadful call from my mum to tell me that my cousin, John, had been found dead that morning. He had suffered what looked like a fatal blood clot, completely out the blue, and his wife and three kids were obviously devastated. What a switch. First my aunt was consoling my mum, and now the reverse; and Aunt Janet wasn't as lucky.

I was filled with what I suppose must be survivor's guilt, but I resolved to make sure my second chance would serve both John and me.

I had some serious living to do.

***

Big Pete, friend – The Date

I spent a month with Corinne one day… here's how it went!

There are two types of people who visit people in hospital. There's the 'I've got to visit someone in hospital' types and the 'I've got to visit someone in hospital' type. Now both types sound the same, but are very different. The first go there out of a bizarre sense of duty. They go for either one of two reasons: either go before the patient gets home so they don't get talked about for not visiting; or go before the patient dies, again so they don't get talked about.

The other type of 'got to goes' are mainly nosey bastards who don't want to miss out on anything! Let's face it, nobody goes hospital-visiting because they like it!

To say that Cor wasn't keen to be in hospital and would like to be somewhere else, would be putting it mildly! During the war, the Japanese used to torture Scottish soldiers by putting on Jimmy Shand records after nailing their boots to the floor so they couldn't tap their feet! If they were about now, they would put Cor in a hospital bed and tell her to stay there! It is the ultimate torture.

One day during visiting, after Corinne had had her amputations, we were talking about the boredom factor of being in hospital; everything was discussed, even jumping out the window! Cor, of course, would have wanted to go first, which would then have ended up with me being on a murder charge, as I would have bottled out of the jump, but I would have had to help her to the window etc, etc. It wouldn't have looked good on me!

Having exhausted loads of different ideas, we decided just to ask if Cor could get out for the afternoon. Like visiting… except outside! The Doctors and Staff were unsure about this at first, but I told them about my medical background – porter in the Southern General, and apprentice soap boy at the Rottenrow Maternity Hospital. I had barely got into my Fire Brigade experiences when they said I was good to go – something about the sooner, the better! Didn't quite catch all of it, but they certainly seemed impressed!

The date was set for that Wednesday afternoon. I was to pick Corinne up at the hospital and take her out for lunch. What could possibly go wrong?

Wednesday came around quickly (as it was actually Tuesday when we asked). Cor was waiting for me outside – did I mention her lack of patience? (As the lift wasn't working, I often wondered how she got the wheelchair down the stairs, but decided not to go there!)

Things didn't start well as Cor wanted to drive the wheelchair, but me being a man, I knew it was really my job. Anyway, we decided to sort this out with Rock/Paper/Scissors. I should have won; perhaps with hindsight, arm-wrestling would have been the better choice. Did I tell you her competitive spirit is matched only by her lack of patience?

So, finally, off we went. With all the 'bits' taken off Cor, the hospital diet, and the fact that she couldn't open any of her sweeties, she was a bit like a Japanese Racing Snake. In fact, it was said if she got any thinner she would only need one eye!

Her lack of weight soon became a problem, as she was slipping out of the wheelchair. I told her if she fell out the chair I wasn't going to pick her up. You could see the whole thing unravelling: 'What are you doing, mate?' 'Oh, I'm just picking up this girl who fell oot the wheelchair.' 'Where's her legs?' 'Cut Off!' 'Where's her hands?' 'Cut off!' 'Well, her luck's no taking a turn fur the better with you turning up!' Next scene, everybody's in the A & E Department and the Police are involved!

Fortunately, Cor had a bra on. (Why? I have no idea, but we managed to harness her to the wheelchair with it! Baraaa!

ANOTHER THING about women losing weight in hospital... I don't go for the 'poor wee soul, she's lost so much weight' thing – I take the 'lucky cow, she always wanted to be a size 6' route! I was thinking of opening a weight loss clinic and running it in a hospital. Everyone would be successful, as everyone loses weight in a hospital (except the nurses, that is... Ha, just kidding!).

So, on we moseyed, down the High Street. Some workies were sitting having their lunch on the pavement. I can still see their faces when I told them to watch their toes as we squeezed by, and Cor chipped in, 'Yes, look what happened to me when I didn't get my feet out the way quick enough!' Did I tell you that Cor's black humour is only matched by her lack of patience and competitiveness?

We finally reached our destination – it wasn't really, but I wasn't going any further, the bra strap looked like it was going to go any minute, and it had taken us as hour to go five minutes down the street! We found that we were at Glasgow Cathedral, so we decided to go in.

There were two paths – one a smooth pavement and one cobble stones. Cor requested the cobble stones. I have no idea why, but it appeared to make her happy – perhaps the same way that sitting on a washing machine on a spin cycle can make women happy – or so I've heard!

There was a disabled entrance, but not for Cor. Did I tell you that her stubbornness is matched only by her lack of patience? No, we had to use the same door as everyone else; the one with the stairs. Luckily, there were some Italian students there. My Italian is a bit rusty, but after I had told them I had ordered my trousers from Belgium and my dog could ride a bike, they seemed happy to help. Corinne's entrance into the Cathedral was like Cleopatra's entrance into Rome, with six handsome Italian men carrying her shoulder-high into the church.

This came to an abrupt end when told by a man: 'Eh, you cannae dae that!'

'Who says?' I queried.

Stuck for a moment, he then replied, 'The Boss.'

'Fair enough,' I replied, 'I ain't gonna argue with GOD!'

We left, using the disabled lift, which turned out to be working and not disabled at all! The man followed us to guide us through the safety procedures – the 18cm drop was not something I would have liked to have attempted on my own! Thank the Lord for Health and Safety!

Now we had finally made it to the Cafe! (Over the cobbles again! Just saying!) Into the Café we went. As with most places nowadays, it was wheelchair-friendly, so after knocking chairs and tables all over the place and running over toes galore, we settled down totally in the way of everybody!

Certain things not to do on a date – Don't order Spag Bol wearing a white shirt. Another good tip (which is totally irrelevant to the date story), don't sneeze when you are hiding! Another thing NOT to do is order a coffee in a cup whose previous life was a Terracotta Warrior's helmet – especially if you are with someone with no hands! As I didn't want to take Cor back to the hospital scalded by coffee, I did what anyone else in my position would do… I ignored the situation!!

Never one to be outdone, Cor tackled the giant cup of coffee. Her tenacity is only matched by her lack of patience, competitiveness, stubbornness and black humour! To go with the coffee, we had cream cakes. I was amazed at how many times I managed to miss her mouth, but hit her nose bang-on! Cor's temper is only matched by her blah, blah, blah.

The 'date' was finally over and it was time to go back to the real world! For me, that meant back in the car and home; for Cor, back to hospital for more tests and more challenges, all of which she tackled head-on.

She is truly remarkable, and we both learned something that day. Corinne learned that you can buy second-hand false teeth at the Barras – and I learned that if anyone was going to beat the massive challenges that were ahead, it was the skinny burd with cream on her nose!

Cor 999!

Colin, Dad

As Cor recovered, she was told that they
were transferring her to the Glasgow
Royal Infirmary Canniesburn Unit for
surgery. At this point we had had no
discussions with the surgeons about how
much of her hands and feet would require to be amputated.
We had hoped that it would be 'just' some fingers and toes.
So it was a complete shock to Cor when the doctor, doing
his morning rounds, announced to his entourage that Ms.
Hutton was to have her hands and lower legs amputated.

Cor phoned me in a state of complete shock, in floods of
tears. At the end of that phone call, I don't know who was
crying the most. My little girl was all on her own, with
no-one to comfort her during this traumatic time. David,
her mum and I went straight to her bedside.

The doctor had assumed that Cor was aware of this deci-
sion. We asked for a second opinion, and David did some
research, as we wanted the very best surgeon possible to
carry out this task. It transpired that Professor Andrew
Hart was undoubtedly the man for the job, and we were all
relieved and pleased that we had got the best for Cor.

One thing that Cor did not like was that she had to be
lifted from her bed by a 'crane and sling', which — in a
hospital gown — did nothing for her dignity. Hospital
staff, for health and safety reasons, are not allowed to lift
patients from bed to chair/wheelchair. Family were able to
visit at any time, so when David and I were there, we
lifted her and sat her on the chair. Health and Safety did
not apply to us.

The first time Cor was allowed out of hospital was for Rory's first day at school. Soon after that, we got our girl home.

I doubt that all the NHS contributions that I have paid over the 50 years of my working life would have covered the cost of Cor's treatment. Thank you, thank you, NHS.

A few days after Corinne's amputations, she said to me, 'Dad, I am not going to be disabled. I promise that whatever I could do before, I am going to do again.'

This showed me the courage and mental determination that would see her through the rocky road that lay ahead.

***

Doreen, Mum

Corinne was transferred to Glasgow Royal Infirmary, to see what they could do with her black hands and feet, but it became obvious that she was going to lose some fingers and toes.

The day after her admission there, I was in the gym about 9am when there was a call over the loudspeaker for me. My heart plummeted and I ran out. It was Colin, my husband, in tears. He said that Corinne had called in hysterics. During the ward round, the consultant had told everyone that Corinne was to have her hands and feet amputated in two days. But this was the first time that this had been said! We had all thought that they would be able to save some bits.

We rushed into hospital, where the poor girl was distraught — and no wonder. As far as we knew, there

had been no discussion. In fairness, the nursing staff were furious and there were lots of apologies, as the consultant taking the ward round had thought Corinne knew.

After we had exhausted all second and third opinions, Corinne herself decided to go ahead; by this time her hands and feet had turned black, were like rocks, and were shocking her every time she had to look at them. Colin seemed to understand this better than me, as I kept thinking they would get better or that, at worst, she might only lose some fingers.

The day of her amputations was awful. When we got in to see her, her limbs were visible through polythene bags with drains fitted, and looked so awful I could have murdered the person who had done this to my beautiful daughter. It looked as if they had cut her up for soup bones.

This was the start of a terrible time for Corinne. She could do nothing for herself and was so frustrated. She hated to be lifted in a harness, and her brothers were very useful for lifting and laying (which was not allowed).

My friends all rallied round and looked for gadgets that might help — a few of which she used. Scott Campbell downloaded loads of talking books for her, but we didn't understand that if she fell asleep she couldn't find the page again, so a very highly qualified Plastics nurse had to help her. I'm not sure that was what they were trained for!

David continued visiting after work every night, and the staff were so good they allowed him to stay until she was ready to sleep. We tried to ensure there was someone there after 2pm, 1-2pm being Russell's time, until 8pm bedtime, David's slot!

Kate had a full time job organising the visiting schedule, but she was great at pointing out to people that Corinne wasn't strong enough to have a lot of visitors, and didn't like to fall asleep when her visitors were there. Although it wasn't allowed, I think the staff were happy to have us there at mealtimes, as it saved their time feeding her.

None of us can comprehend how awful it is not to be able to go to the toilet, and even wipe yourself, when you have no hands. David spent 24 hours with his hands taped up to try and find a way to do these personal things.

All the operations meant more tracheotomies, which of course meant she couldn't speak again. David was sitting by her bed one night when she was trying to tell him something that he couldn't understand. Eventually, it dawned on him that a boy who had been at school with them was a designer of bionic parts. This started David on a new line of research into bionics,

It was about this time that David and Scott starting talking about setting up a charity, mainly to give Corinne an interest, and because they realised that there was a lot missing in the after-care of patients who have experienced a terrible trauma like this. There were apparently only three other people in Scotland who had suffered something similar.

When Corinne had the operation that entailed stitching what was left of her hand into her stomach for three weeks, she couldn't move or turn. It was awful for her. One night she was so broken that she cried for ages, couldn't settle, and was terrified. I said I would stay the night and be there if she needed me. The charge nurse was wonderful, and about 11pm she insisted I go home and said she would take my place.

That was a terrible night for me, too. I had to leave my daughter in a hospital with strangers, having gone through so much. I can't express how it felt to sit there and look at my poor mutilated child, covered in scars and bandages, completely helpless, and I was unable to help.

One day I went in and she wasn't in her room. She had gone to the physiotherapy department, so I went there — and she was upright! She had two blow-up legs on and, with a physiotherapist on each side of her, she managed to move a few steps. She was over the moon! And I was in tears again.

In mid-August Rory was due to start school, and Corinne was determined to be there. She told the staff that there was really no choice in this, that she was going... and she did. Davy scooped her up into a wheelchair to avoid nurses using a hoist, and she escaped for the day.

It was as if the whole village had turned out to see her; she was surrounded by people, many of whom had gone to school with her, or with one of the family.

I was so proud of her and the way she spoke to everyone. And Rory was as pleased as punch as he pushed her about in her wheelchair. She felt that she was again Rory's mum and, by the time we left, she was exhausted but happy.

***

Elaine, friend and Rory's Head Teacher

The first day of the school year is, for me, the most important day of the school year; the day which parents and pupils antici-

pate the most. I love seeing all of the pupils dressed smartly in their new uniforms, and excited to begin a new year. As a Head Teacher, it is the day when I feel most 'under the microscope'; when I feel the most pressure to get it right.

This was never more so than on Rory's first day of school. I remember going to visit Corinne in hospital the night before; it was the first time I had seen her since the amputation operations. I was adamant that Rory's first day wouldn't be the first time we had met since the operation, as I wanted to be able to deal with the situation personally and privately with her before we were in a packed playground filled with pupils and parents.

We spent the visit talking about how we hoped the day would go, and putting plans in place to make it as easy as possible for both Corinne and Rory — parking at the school gate; meeting in a corner of the playground, so as the focus remained on the Primary 1 children, and Corinne had time to be with Rory and focus on him. We put a considerable amount of time into planning the day, then I discussed with staff how it would run (with military precision!) and briefed them to just be 'normal' with Corinne; casual, informal, and relaxed, as they would always have been before.

I felt so proud that day that it went so well; the focus remained on Rory (as was our priority,) and Corinne was able to share this momentous day with him. It was wonderful to see Rory just the same as every other P1 — excited to start his first day of school, with his mum by his side.

After that, I checked in with him every morning after he first started school, and texted Corinne with updates and *photos so that she would still feel a part of his first months at school. I clearly remember I spoke to him the morning after we heard she was going to be discharged from hospital, and asked him if he had any news to share with me. His answer was so poignant and perfect: 'Mummy's coming home, FOREVER!'*

A couple of other stories spring to mind. I remember visiting Corinne's nephew, Huck, in class the day after we heard that Corinne was being transferred back to Glasgow from Leicester. I spoke to his class teacher and said, 'Huck got some wonderful news yesterday. Would you like to tell your teacher, Huck?' To which he answered, 'Yes! My grandma got chocolate cake for her birthday!'

Another was when Corinne came along to our Hallowe'en Disco, and almost immediately a pupil walked across and pretty much asked, 'Where are your hands?' The way she answered so calmly, explaining so well what had happened, was a testament to her positive attitude and wonderful way of dealing with all that was happening to her

***

Kate, sister-in-law and great mate

In the dark days after the amputations, it was our job to keep Cor's spirits up and be super-positive.

When Corinne decided that she would like to start having visitors, the doctors said okay, but we weren't to have too many people at once as she was still exhausted. So I tried to be helpful and to stagger everyone's visiting times to spread the visitors out during the course of the day. Obviously that

worked really well – NOT! They were all so desperate to see her that they just came anyway, and complained to her that they would have been there sooner and more often but it was hard getting past the 'gate-keeper'!

Even although Cor was still very delicate and trying to get her head round everything that had happened, the poor soul wasn't allowed much time to wallow when the girls were around. We'd give her a couple of minutes of tears and then it was all business and move on to the next thing! (It was actually rather hypocritical of us, as it took months for us to be able to go for a girlie night out and not have some-one end up in tears.)

Just because she was in hospital, we wouldn't let stand-ards slip, and sometimes her room resembled a beauty salon with all the make-up flying around that we insisted she put on. Unfortunately, one day Davy got there before us and offered to help her, and she spent the day looking like 'Aunt Sally'! She was not best pleased when she found out, but Davy laughed all day.

Hair-washing also proved to be a bit of a challenge and, until we got the hang of it, quite often the room was wetter than her hair.

She asked me to tint her eyelashes for her one day and, even though I could do it, I hadn't done it for a while and was slightly nervous. Cor obviously picked up on that and said, 'I hope you know what you're doing, as there's not much left of me and I can't afford to lose an eye as well!' No pressure.

Eventually the nurses turned a blind to the steady flow of visitors, but the first time she was sneaked out of the hospi-

tal was a real coup! It was only for a coffee next door, but it was something 'normal' to do, and for a few minutes she was free.

She had been out of her room a couple of times, but the school summer holidays were over and the kids were going back to school. Rory was starting Primary One — and no-one wants to miss that.

It was brilliant to see her there, and Rory was SO pleased to have his mum there. Cor said she felt that for the first time since she had been ill, Rory saw her as 'Mum' again that day, and it was a huge turning point for her.

***

Emma, sister-in-law and friend:
My Worst Moment

I will always remember the day I got the call — sitting in work — from my husband, Scott, to say I needed to come home because we had to get on a plane from Dubai to say goodbye to his sister, Corinne. We had been told the night before that she had been admitted to hospital with pneumonia, but that she was okay. How did it turn into a call to say she was dying? She survived and she was still with us, but the hard stuff was still to come for her — and for us.

I remember the day we got the call to say that Corinne had to have quadruple amputations... how did that happen? Why? There had been many dark days between this phone call and the first one, but this was almost worse. She had survived and had been through enough, so why this? But it had to happen to keep her with us forever.

The first time I saw Corinne since she had been on the ECMO machines, was in a hospital bed, and she was a shadow of her former self. We'd had to travel back to Dubai and return again. Her hands and feet were wrapped up, but her black fingers and toes were visible. I was not shocked by this, because I had built myself up to cope with it... and I did. I think I coped so well because Corinne did. How could I not cope, seeing the strength coming from her? I would have been ashamed if I hadn't been able to find the strength to be normal and talk about the weather, when she was doing so well ... on the outside, anyway. My moment was yet to come.

The day Corinne had her operations, we sat around and drank tea; lots of tea. We took calls from friends and family all around the world and people we didn't even know, sending love and prayers. The time came later that night when we could take turns to go and see her. I was confident that I was going to be okay; I had seen her with black feet and black hands, and I'd coped.

I drove to the hospital with Scott and Kate, and we chatted and tried to speak of anything else but what we were about to see. Until we pulled up outside. They asked me if I was ready; I asked them if they were ready; we were all ready — or so I thought.

We walked into the ICU ward, which was big. There was a long corridor; well, it seemed to be long at the time, leading to the corner where Corinne was positioned in the unit. We turned the corner and I froze. I couldn't breathe. I literally couldn't breathe.

Scott and Kate had to keep walking, as she was facing us,

but I had to swiftly turn back around the corner to compose myself. All I could see was that half of the bed was filled with her legs, but where had the rest of her gone? It was real, this had really happened. I took some deep breaths and made a quick recovery. I knew she was probably on so much pain relief she wouldn't even notice my absence or me arriving a few moments later than the others, but I couldn't take any more time. I didn't have the right to be weak, I didn't have the right to be crying when someone I loved so much needed her family and needed us to be strong.

I got to the bed and Scott and Kate were doing a great job laughing at her jokes. She was cracking jokes. I'm not sure if she remembers, but she was making fun of herself, flashing around her open wounds on her hands that were wrapped in clear plastic dressings. This was also hard to see the first time, but I had dealt with my shock earlier; it was now time for me to be strong for her, and for my husband.

This was all bad enough for me to cope with, but Scott was watching his sister go through this, and had to stand by and watch, and there was nothing he could do to help her.

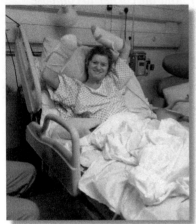

Look no hands!

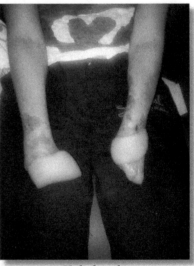

Ugly hands

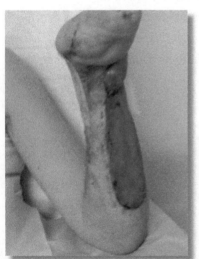

My left hand

Scott Campbell visits

Dad, Rory & Cooper

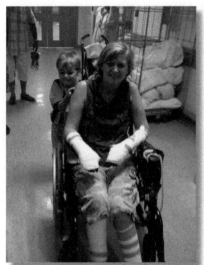

Proud Rory

First day at school

CHAPTER 5
HOME TIME

I left hospital on 4th September, 2013 — missing two legs and two hands — to start to rebuild my life. I couldn't do anything for myself, and depended so much on my family and friends. I'm a very proud, independent, and determined person, so it was very hard to accept the fact that I needed help. But they made it easy for me, and never complained or made me feel a nuisance.

On my second day home, my brothers obviously felt the need to make me laugh, so we concocted a plan to get me and my wheelchair onto the roof of Davy's Land Rover for a photo op. (Well, of course you would!) With a lot of hilarity, and much pushing and shoving, I got there and was laughing uncontrollably. Until Davy started the engine! He was jesting, but my face must've been a picture. I felt so alive and more like myself than I had done in months, and it was great. My husband was furious, but I wanted to *not* be an invalid for a moment, and it was brilliant.

I pushed for daily physiotherapy visits so that I could learn to walk quickly, and my dutiful brother, Davy, picked me up every morning and took me to WestMARC at Glasgow Southern General Hospital. There, I arrived second every day, beaten consistently by Seamus, my tough, determined, and very, very kind fellow amputee. Every day Seamus made sure my biscuit was removed from the wrapper at break time and the sugar packet was opened for my tea. He topped me by having hands, you see!

I met many characters in physio, and really appreciated being amongst folks similar to me. The range of emotions and how we all dealt with our trauma was very varied as well. I always had my 'happy mask' on, but there were some days that it was all a bit of much for me. The majority of amputees had circulation problems from illnesses such as diabetes, and the average age was high. There were a few, though, like me, who had just suffered from bad luck infections or accidents.

I was constantly frustrated with one physiotherapist who kept knocking down my hopes and targets by telling me, 'You're called patient for a reason.' I wasn't patient. But I bet the ex-servicemen in physio weren't told to be 'patient' and had their expectations crushed.

I felt the physio's job was to push the individual according to their ability, and not set limits. I now know there are no limits, and you can achieve anything you want to with enough determination.

You can even wear high-heeled prosthetics if you're prepared to work hard at learning to walk on them. The minute I was told I wouldn't ever wear a heel again, that was always going to happen! Be encouraging, not discouraging!

I was thrilled at the rate of progress I was able to make, though, and pretty proud of myself. That feeling was shared by my family and friends, who could see that the old Corinne wasn't too far away. Every day had a 'first' or an improvement, and the learning curve was steep and hard but very rewarding.

Unfortunately, this enthusiasm wasn't shared by my husband, and he cast a negative shadow over my first months of being home. Every positive achievement, every 'first', everything I was proud of myself for, he seemed to pour scorn on. He told me I wanted a pat on the back for everything I did. And maybe I did. But maybe I just wanted him to see that I wouldn't always be a burden, and for him to share my excitement. Sadly, that wasn't to be, and he moved out after six months.

Looking back at my time in hospital, Russell's visits had mostly been a time of negativity for me. He would tell me how hard it was at home, and how much pressure he was under. I was already feeling very guilty for not being there for him and Rory, and he didn't try to make me feel any better or pretend that he was coping. Never anything to cheer me up. Sure, he would bring in anything I asked him to, like clothing or toiletries. But I just thought that was typical man stuff.

My friends and family, though, arrived full of ideas and with inspirational videos or articles. For example, Kate would pluck my eyebrows or wash my hair; Mandy brought a digital photo frame loaded with pics from all my friends from our girlie exploits; Mor brought pictures from her twins; and HER husband, Fabio, brought steak sandwiches when my iron level was low. You get the picture.

Maybe I'm only remembering the negative. He actually did do a lot at home when I was discharged from hospital. I remember him spending hours upstairs, ironing or something, when I couldn't get upstairs, so I'd sit alone downstairs. When he came down, I'd have a couple of things I'd been waiting patiently to ask him to do. Perhaps there was something I'd dropped, or a fastening I needed done. He always did it, but there was often a 'tut' or a sigh along with it, which just made me feel like I was a real nuisance.

Clearly, Russell moving out was a kick I didn't need at that time. But instantly, I felt the negativity was gone; instantly, my friends felt at ease coming round; and, oddly, I felt less alone. But I was shattered for Rory. He'd been through so much in the last six months and I wanted to protect him from any more. We didn't ever argue in front of him, but things were very strained for a while and I sensed he'd picked up on that. I'd already had one failed marriage and, although it wasn't my choice, felt a real failure then; now I had to face a second failure.

I knew I would struggle practically and I was in a mess financially, but I needed to surround myself with positive things and people, as the risk of crashing was very real and never far from my mind. I was determined I would damn well prove myself.

That's when I discovered REAL wealth, in the shape of the most wonderful family and friends, and the most fantastic wee boy. Rory is the main reason for me doing and achieving anything. I can't allow him to see anything but a strong, able mum.

I had people getting me up and dressed; taking me to the plentiful hospital appointments; bringing me food parcels; trying to help me find clothes that fitted my new size and could go over my fairly chunky new legs; making sure I would be safely in bed for the night; dragging me to the gym to build my muscles back up; making sure Rory was looked after; and making sure I got to go out and do things that made me feel 'alive'.

From them to the many rekindled friendships and the complete strangers who wanted to help 'fix me', I can't even begin to explain what it meant to me, and how it helped me find MY feet. How lucky was I to have that network open to me?

One week after starting physiotherapy, I had new prosthetics legs. I was very frustrated at the rate at which the physios encouraged me to progress (or not). To be fair, they were very concerned with protecting the healing wounds on my legs, but I had healthy wounds where others struggled with circulation issues.

First, I had to learn to stand up and sit down, and did it 50 times or so a day. My muscles had vanished and I was very weak, and the most basic act of raising myself out of a seated position was really tough.

After baby steps, I was terrified to find how uncomfortable these prosthetics were. I could sustain them for just a few minutes a day initially, and couldn't believe I would ever get to the point of wearing them all day. But, again, determination prevailed and each day I added a minute or two to the wearing time. After a few weeks with a zimmer, I moved on to elbow crutches (I obviously couldn't hold onto normal ones) with my trusted wheelchair always nearby to rest in when I couldn't stand any longer.

I would have to take my new legs off for relief, and there was more than one time Rory would take them away to play with them, leaving me having to 'find my feet', literally! Crutches are like weapons! Wherever I leaned on them, they fell onto me or, worse, someone else, but I really depended on them and we moved into winter where I was constantly at risk of slipping or falling. Four months later, at a Christmas party, I put my crutches to the side when arriving and didn't touch them again until I left to go home — and I didn't miss them. So Davy stopped me taking them the next day, and they were never used again.

In fact, I've found I could learn to do anything I wanted to do. Almost always, I worried that a new thing, a new action, a new event would be too difficult for me. And the first time at anything was stressful, filled with nerves, slow or clumsy. Everything became a new puzzle where I needed to work out the right method for me.

This has all been done without any meaningful help from Occupational Therapists, I might add. Later I was to discover what a good OT could do for me, and Steph has restored my faith in their purpose. But previously, when I needed it most, I got no meaningful help.

My theory was that I was so determined to learn that they just left me to it. Or perhaps because I refused to convert my house until I knew what I needed, they thought they were redundant. One OT sat my friend Mor and I down and took two hours to go through a list of activities to see what I could and couldn't do. Everything from zips and laces to door handles and kettles. We assumed she would later come back with ideas on how I could actually do them. Nope, nothing. When Mor asked her next time we saw her, she said that Corinne could ask if she wanted help. So what was the point of the two-hour list?

I read a book by Jamie Andrews around that time. He was a mountaineer who lost his limbs to frostbite. His OT had taken him daily to a simulated kitchen and had him open drawers, turn on taps, etc, to help him learn. When I told my OT, she told me there was one in their rehab unit. Well, who exactly was using it? If not me — busy young(ish) mum, having lost her hands and legs — then who? I was too appalled at her to ask for anything at that point. Useless!

(Jamie is now a friend of Finding Your Feet and has supervised and advised us on climbing and skiing clubs. His sister swims with us and says I'm a better swimmer than him!)

We worked out as a family how to do many things. For example, to use a belt to hook through a grab handle and swing from my wheelchair into the car seat, or using Velcro straps to hook my arms through to open the fridge.

My father-in-law built me a ramp for my wheelchair to get in the front door. It would have taken the system months to fit one, by which time I had moved on and no longer needed it!

***

Scott called one day to say that a prosthetist in Dubai had heard of our situation and wanted to help. Before I could get to meet Charl Stenger, Mum and Dad had been to see him with Scott and they were all very excited about his ideas, even getting emotional at what he could do for me.

I flew out for a cycle event which Scott had entered a team into to raise funds for Finding Your Feet. There were 50 participants, including eight from Scotland. They raised £60,000 that day, and at the evening event and I was like Queen Muck getting all the attention!

That seemed like a good time to book to see Charl, and both Davy and Scott Campbell wanted to meet him, too. I left that day, having been cast for new legs that would hugely improve my posture and walking – and they did. What a star!

***

In Dubai, Scott and Emma have a beautiful house, but the stairs are steep marble and curl right round, making it difficult for me to walk up. At first, I was only comfortable at night relaxing with my legs off, and I would dread putting them back on to go to bed. Rather than that, Scott offered most nights to carry me up. Although it was helpful and kind, I found it shameful and I was embarrassed. Even more so one night when I did manage to walk up in my new clever legs. I'd just collected them that day and was so pleased with them. Prosthetist Charl told me that the pin attached to my silicon liner clipped into a ratchet system, and would be so strong that they could hang me upside down! Superb… or so I thought!

After Scott had said good night and left me, I pressed the button that would release the ratchet. One released the leg easily, but one didn't. I tried over and over again, wondering what I was doing wrong. I pulled and pushed, twisted and turned, but could not release this one leg. What should I do? I had one leg on and one off, stopping me from walking or crawling. My young nephews were sleeping, so I didn't want to shout and wake them, also knowing that Scott would be sound and wouldn't hear me, anyway!

Sleeping in a prosthetic leg is not a good option and I was panicking. Fortunately, Emma popped her head in the door and, seeing my distress, tried to help. She pulled and pushed, twisted and turned, too, but didn't do any better than me, but we did laugh at our predicament. She went to wake Scott (requiring quite some persistence), who came in, half asleep, assuming we were being silly girls.

In actual fact, I'm more practical than both my brothers so I doubted he'd do any better. He resorted to brute strength, which he certainly does better than me, but I reminded him of Charl's words that he could hang me upside down and I wouldn't come off this leg!

It didn't stop him trying, and I was hung upside down. Emma sat on me to stop me sliding while he pulled at my leg, then he hit my leg with a shoe but nothing was releasing that pin.

I had been given a spray to clean the liners, and Emma came up with a suggestion of squirting it into the tiniest of gaps between the liner and my own stump, trying to lubricate my leg enough to slip out of the liner; this seemed plausible. Unfortunately, the liner was so tightly fitted to my own leg and was still inside the prosthetic leg, so we were only able to get tiny amounts in with every squirt, whilst trying to pull the silicon away from my skin.

I could feel movement, though, as the liquid was forced down inside the liner, and after 90 minutes of squirting and wriggling the fluid down, my leg eventually slipped out of both the liner and its attached prosthetic leg. Relief!

Charl apologised the next day when we discovered a flaw in the ratchet, which was quickly repaired. He also suggested that should it happen again, a swift knock on the leg around the area of the pin might knock the pin back into place, or that lubrication was a handy thing to keep nearby.

My bed now has a mallet and a bottle of Fairy Liquid permanently placed underneath, just in case!

***

Doreen, Mum

When Corinne finally got her first pair of legs, my sister-in-law Margaret and I were requested to go on a course on learning how to walk with her, which was rubbish as I had been walking with her every day. But it gave us all a laugh. Part of the problem was that they hadn't dealt with anyone in Corinne's position, as the other two patients had come from Edinburgh and had not been allowed home until they could do things like opening an envelope.

We then started going to the gym every morning, where Scott Campbell patiently went through her exercises with her. Being Corinne, though, she soon became fed up with being helped and watched, and insisted that she could do things by herself. I would hide behind pillars or machines watching, or have the instructor positioned nearby. I was utterly terrified that she would break.

One of the little funnies was that I had to take Corinne for an 'assessment' to ascertain that she was (whisper it!) disabled. The poor person who was carrying this out was mortified. She would ask things like, could she dress herself, and Corinne would answer 'yes'. I would then have to say that she could, but it took about three hours! The lady said

she had never come across this before, someone with such profound disabilities trying hard to prove she was fine.

One question asked, 'How far can you walk in the morning?' I answered, 'Can't walk. No legs.' The next question was, 'How far can you walk in the afternoon?' I answered, 'Still can't walk, still no feckin' legs.' My Irish sister-in-law was helping me, and she reckoned that Brendan O'Carroll, of Mrs. Brown's Boys, would have been proud of that reply.

Finding my feet

High-heeled prosthetics

New wheelchair

The best way to
travel in a Land Rover

CHAPTER 6
BACK TO BASICS

Learning to do things for myself was a very steep, but very positive climb-back to being the independent person I had always been. But I was determined to do everything I could previously, if at all possible.

Obviously, walking was first on my list, but before that I had to learn to get my legs on and off by myself. That's quite difficult with no hands, and at first I needed help. But independence was vital for me, and I spent days and days just standing up from a seated position and sitting back down again.

My previously decent muscle tone had now all gone. It seems so basic, but that was such a hard thing for me to do that I would almost launch myself up and forward, which kept my physio on her toes!

Transferring to and from the wheelchair/bed/sofa also needed a lot of practice, and I took my little electric chair with me everywhere. I had to sit helpless, watching my poor mum struggle to separate the seat from the base and the battery, then load the considerably heavy base into the boot of her car, and this upset me every time. Quite often, if I knew someone would be with me, or space was limited in the car, I would take my little lightweight wheel-chair, but that required someone to push me. Once, Mor pushed me to her car then opened the door for me, but in those few seconds, I'd free-wheeled down the road a bit!

My lack of hands was particularly frustrating, like when I needed to lock and unlock a key in the door. I bought key-holders that gave me a bigger area to grip and would have been great, but I had no sense of pressure. So I would turn it when it had stuck, and the key frequently snapped in the lock, requiring new locks to be fitted on a few occasions. My hands also had no sense of hot or cold for about 18 months, so scorching them in the kitchen or on a mug was pretty common. I would also frequently be told off when someone felt them freezing while I was outside. But I just didn't feel it.

Six months after leaving hospital, I walked a mile with a bunch of those same kids from Lochwinn-och Primary, Rory's school. To save us from crossing roads and traffic worries, we chose to walk around George Square in Glasgow city centre enough times to make one mile. We chatted, laughed, and did sums all the way so that the kids didn't miss their school-ing! Imagine celebrating walking one mile, but those little things meant so much — and a positive event took away the risk of negativity setting in.

Dealing with mascara and champagne glasses were also early lessons. Needs must, you understand!

Before leaving, Russell had given me skiing lessons with Disability UK, as a Christmas present, which was actually a very thoughtful thing to buy me. So I booked in for my first lesson at the local indoor ski slope six months after leaving hospital. I had skied since I was 12 or so, and was therefore a pretty experienced and confident skier. I loved really pushing myself, and had taken lessons previously with Scott to learn powder skiing and bumps; I loved the speed and the effort it took.

Let me tell you, that was nothing to learning to do it all on artificial legs! First, I had to take my legs off, force them into the ski boots (with a little help), and then put them back on again. I walked like a spaceman and was obviously a little nervous. My legs wouldn't go where I wanted them to and I was really nervous, but I managed to climb up the lower hill and ski down without falling. (Getting back up from a fall seemed impossible!)

By my third lesson I was on a ski tow and managing turns pretty well, but the technique that the instructor wanted me to try for was quite alien to me. In fact, she told me that 50% of her job would be teaching me to ski on prosthetics, and 50% would be getting rid of years of bad habits. Charming!

Driving was high on my priority list to get my independence back, but I wasn't sure that I would be allowed. I waited six months for an assessment in Edinburgh and was so nervous, but so keen, too. My prosthetist, Vincent, and I had discussed whether my legs could cope with the pedals. My hands were going to be under enough pressure to steer, indicate, etc, so I felt that having to cope with hand controls to brake and accelerate would be a bit too much.

Vincent explained how my thighs would produce the pressure down through my prosthetics and onto the pedal, and that many amputees used foot pedals. I had practised a little with Davy, driving his big hard Jeep, so I knew I could do it, but I just hoped the authorities would agree.

I arrived at Astley Ainslie Hospital and was first taken through a range of mental tests and puzzles to assess my attention span and mental status. One was to draw a clock face with all the numbers on; I struggled to hold a pen, so that was an amusing but frustrating one. After that, I was put in a car 'shell' and asked to brake on demand and accelerate at different rates. So far so good.

They flashed several lights across the windscreen and asked me to count them in the one second they were lit. This had little to do with my amputations and I was confused as to why it was relevant, but I guess they deal with many physical and mental situations so I had to just get through it.

After passing these tests, I was allowed into a real car; automatic, but that was probably sensible. It was explained that prosthetic legs can get caught amongst the pedals and it's not often easy to be aware of it or to get unstuck. Accordingly, they asked me to try left foot braking, leaving my right foot to control the acceleration. That involved a couple of whiplash moments, but it was surprisingly easy to get used to.

My right hand, at first, was put into a leather glove that had a pin protruding from it, which slotted into a ratchet attached to the steering wheel and allowed me to turn it safely.

After that, another prosthetic-type arrangement was attached to the steering wheel. I would have accepted whatever they told me to use, in order to be allowed to drive again, but these were quite restrictive and uncomfortable as I could never relax my arm (at traffic lights, for example), and additionally they were hard for me to get into by myself. When my assessor tried a third option, I was so excited. It was basically a foam steering wheel cover which gave me extra grip, but allowed me freedom to move my hands as I wanted.

I pleaded with her to allow me this, and after an hour driving around Edinburgh, she agreed to give me the authority to go to DVLA and ask for my licence back. But only after a few driving lessons to perfect that new braking action. Result! What a feeling of relief and excitement, and such a big step for Rory and me to become mobile without all the helpers who had been kind enough to transport us around. Freedom at last! And one more nail in the coffin of disability that I was determined to shake off.

***

I was put in touch with a swimming instructor by a friend, Julie, who said Andrew Jackson coached disabled paralympians to swim and he wanted to help. I was terrified of getting in the pool, but I knew I wanted to conquer that fear and be able to take Rory swimming again. Again, the first time was scary and I firstly had to work out how to get to the pool. To get my clothes off meant taking my legs off, costume on, and then putting my legs back on and walking to the side of the pool. How would I then get my legs off again? Where could I sit? How would I get down from the seat without legs? How would I get to the pool edge and how would I get in? And out? How would I get my legs on whilst wet? All these puzzles needed to be solved.

At first I resorted to the wheelchair, but how could I get in and out of it if I was wet and slippy? Now I walk to the poolside, trying to turn a blind eye to how strange I look, as my shoes have to stay on my legs. A few times I've forgotten that and gone to the pool in swimsuit and over-the-knee boots! It's a great fashion statement, and quite an eye-catcher.

That first time, though, I wriggled to the poolside and looked nervously at the water and wondered whether I would just sink on entry. But Andrew was there for me and let me adjust to my new set-up and the very different buoyancy issues — my stumps wanted to float to the surface, oddly! He taught me how to use my whole arm to pull, in order to compensate for lack of hands, and I learned how little my legs could do to propel me in the water, without feet! It was stressful, embarrassing and exhausting, but I was ecstatic when I got home.

Again, the first time was hard and worrying, but after some extensive coaching from a friend, Chris, using noodles and floats, I can now swim 30 lengths unaided and I can do all three strokes pretty well. Chris also took on the task of trying to save my calf muscles with swimming. Without feet, the calf muscle is redundant, but we felt they offered me padding and circulation benefits, so he set about finding kicking exercises to build them up. And he loved when I suffered from cramp in them. Our gym looks onto the pool and I frequently joke to watchers that I'm off to 'bob' in the pool, to make me feel less self-conscious! The alternative, however, is NOT to swim with my son, and I'd rather be embarrassed than miss out.

All these firsts happened within a very short period of time and while I was still quite weak.

Now I run, ski, cycle, and pretty much have a go at anything suggested to me! I've had flying lessons, and have a few sporting challenges planned. I've carried The Queen's Baton; been invited to the Holyrood garden party; to Downing Street to meet then Prime Minister David Cameron; had lunch with the Scottish First Minister, Alex Salmond — who later resigned, but then I met the new one, Nicola Sturgeon (in fact, she invited some of our young amputees to lunch at Holyrood and was very encouraging of their achievements and plans. I have met a good few celebrities;

and been given an Honorary Doctorate from the University of the West of Scotland. There are many doors opening for me that I thought would be closed.

**

Chris Terris, friend and swimming instructor

Cor: 'Chris, this is weird, I can feel my toes tingle...'

Me: 'Err... Cor, you've not got any toes.'

I have been a swimming instructor for many years, but had never coached anyone with a disability. Cor had mentioned that her calf muscles were wasting away, as they were being under-used in her prosthetic legs. I suggested we could pretty much isolate any muscle in the pool, so why not give that a try.

I never knew Cor before she was ill, and up until this point I had only seen her standing tall and confident in her funky, bright pink prosthetic legs. So, seeing her having to crawl in and out of the pool brought home a sobering reality.

If we didn't know each other particularly well before- hand, we certainly became more 'intimate' as the weeks progressed.

'It's okay, just shove me by the arse,' she would tell me. Fair do's, happy to 'help'.

You've heard of the hit un-pc disability show on Channel 4 called The Last Leg? Well, this was our equivalent — The Last Length.

It was obvious that Cor was a good swimmer, and we adapted strokes and drills to isolate other muscle areas.

For example, we did lots of side stroke as she is stronger down one side than the other, and after a few weeks the physio even commented that there was a little more strength balance coming back. This was incredibly rewarding feedback.

Over the initial weeks we played around with pull-buoys and hand-paddles, however these just became opportunities for supervised drowning. I didn't want Cor to become a statistic and I'm sure David Lloyd, our gym, could do without the paperwork. So we quickly went back to the tried and tested.

Want to know how it feels to swim like Cor? Well, first of all, put a pair of goggles and a nose clip on, with no hands. Then next time you are in the water, tie your legs together at the ankle and make fists with your hands. Now swim 25 lengths freestyle.

Cor, if I slip from my mortal coil before I would like to, you can have any part of me you want. I'm sure you've been eyeing up my lady-like hands anyway!

***

Kate, sister-in-law and great mate

There have been so many 'firsts' for Cor whilst on the road to recovery, that it makes us all realise what we take for granted every day.

Her 'first' set of new legs was a huge deal. Even although they were agony in the beginning, she took great delight in telling me that she'd lied to the prosthetics team that she had been taller than she was before she

had been ill, so her new legs now made her taller than me. That's just not on!

'You laugh or you cry' was a well-used phrase with us, and humour has managed to get us through some crazy situations. Obviously a lot of it was very dark humour, and poor Corinne found herself the subject of some very suspect comments and opportunistic photographs, but it had to be done!

There's not one of us who knows Corinne, who hasn't at one time sat and thought, 'What if that was me?' I'd like to think that I would have dealt with it with the same grace that Corinne has, but it's a big ask and no-one can know unless they are in that situation. It certainly makes us think twice about moaning about any aches and pains, because nothing comes anywhere close to what Corinne has to put up with.

Without doubt, she really is an incredible person, and puts us all to shame with everything that she does these days. She literally never stops, and does everything she did beforehand and much more.

Lots of people have said to me that if it had to happen to anyone, then Corinne was the very one who would cope with it – and they're right. She is a very determined and strong-willed person. Her family are strong-willed and determined people, who fought hard to get the best care possible for her.

Everyone — friends and family — has played a part in getting Cor to where she is today, which is one of the reasons the charity Finding Your Feet was started — to help, amongst other things, people who don't have the

support that Corinne did. She felt embarrassed by all the help she received from family and friends, and hated feeling needy, but she would have been the first person banging on the door if this had happened to someone else.

There really aren't enough words for me to describe how much respect I have for her. For how she has dealt with what she has been through, and how she continues to move forward. And I, for one, am proud to be called her friend – even if it means I have to continue doing things like butterfly-stitching her backside together again after she falls off her bike! But then, what are friends for?

***

Janie, friend: The First Celebration

I have many memories of Corinne's illness and the impact it had on her family and friends. I cannot begin to imagine the pain and worry her family felt, but I can give you a view of how it felt for a friend.

Many memories I cannot consider without being transported back to the awful desperate worry we all had as a constant in our life while we knew our friend was, first of all, fighting for her life, and then battling to rebuild it. She has moved on from this and helped the rest of us to do the same.

That said, most of my memories are of a brave and tough lady who has impressed us all with her determination; stubborn is the best description. If you tell Corinne she cannot do something, she will find a way to do it. She already had that strength in abundance before her illness, across both her work and social life.

Therefore, the memory I would like to share is a good one, in fact a great one, and for me it was the first time I saw our sociable, fun-loving Corinne coming back to us.

In late Sept 2013, we had a 50th birthday party for my husband, Thomas (or Tam, as Corinne calls him). Thomas had debated whether he should go ahead with a party, as it was so soon after Corinne's illness and her resulting amputations. However, around that time the idea of the charity was formulating in the mind of the Hutton family and, keen to do something to support her, Thomas decided to go ahead and have a 'no present rule' and ask the guests to donate to Corinne's charity.

The party was in full swing as we all gathered in our 80s gear, and the charity buckets were filling up nicely, when Corinne arrived with her mum, dad, Kate and David all fussing around her. Of course, as soon as she arrived, we fussed around, too. There was no need for fuss!

At that time, Cor was getting around in an electric wheelchair, and was all dressed in her 80s gear. Thirty minutes after she arrived, Cor asked her dad and David to lift her wheelchair onto the dance floor. And that is where she stayed for the rest of the night, laughing and having fun with her friends; and things were as they should be, as they used to be.

Although it was only the beginning for Cor, and she had hard work and tough times ahead, I knew then she would manage it. I should never have doubted it.

Jump ahead to April 15, 18 months later, and we were in Donegal for my 50th. Corinne walked to the beach, we danced in the bar, and when we were going through security

at Derry Airport, we could not convince security that she could not take her boots off as she had artificial legs!

My final compliment to Corinne is that on a regular basis I forget that she has artificial legs.

I would like to say there is nothing that I can do which she cannot. However, the truth is there are plenty of things she can do that I cannot, e.g. skiing, playing football, cycling around Arran.

That was the case before her illness, and it's the same story now.

***

Doreen, Mum

Corinne was getting brighter by the week, and was determined she would do everything anyone else could do. She had been given skiing lessons at Braehead in Glasgow for her Christmas, and fortunately you have to wait a while to get an appointment. But she had always been an excellent skier, so when she got on the skis, she managed. Again, my heart was in my mouth, and eventually Colin, Rory and I left and went into the shopping centre.

Her exploits since then have been massive, usually involving her poor father doing it with her. She got up, and down, Ben Nevis but couldn't move for days afterwards due to blistered legs. She did a survival trip through Finlayson Estate, and had to change legs for different types of terrain, as one set couldn't get wet — so her dad had to carry the spare set. The last obstacle was to climb a waterfall with the

aid of a rope to pull yourself up. Not easy with no hands. At that point, David appeared in the water and threw her over his shoulder; for once she admitted she was pleased to see him.

In the summertime we were lucky enough to have all four of our grandsons, and their mums, with us at Center Parc, where the only mode of transport is bicycles. While we were there, Corinne and David received an invitation to the Queen's Garden Party at Holyrood.

The day before the event, I pleaded with Corinne to put on her cycling helmet, but was told, 'Oh, for goodness sake, Mother.' Inevitably, she fell off the bike, so she went to the Garden Party with a black eye.

When Corinne was transferred to Glasgow Royal Infirmary, David vowed he would leave no stone unturned to make her as good as we could. A tragedy like this shows you what's important in life, and who your real fiends are. And for my family and friends, I couldn't be more grateful.

One mile walk

'Hands off NHS' protest at Downing Street

Tam's eighties party

With former Prime Minister David Cameron

THE QUEEN'S BATON RELAY
14th June to 23rd July 2014

Abseiling
© Tony Nicoletti

At the velodrome

Sledging

Ski legs

New car © Caroline Stewart

CHAPTER 7
HANDS ON

During my amputations, Professor Hart introduced the possibility of me having hand transplants in the future. I have to confess that I wasn't at all interested; mainly, I think, because I'd been through so many operations. Immune suppressant drugs for the rest of my life was a scary thought when I was still recovering from a very nasty infection which my body hadn't fought very well.

Still, Professor Hart requested that I wasn't to have any more blood transfusions without his knowledge, as this would reduce my chances of being an acceptable transplantee. He raised the subject again a few times over the following weeks, and I still wasn't at all attracted to the idea. But it was clear that he was.

In March, Dad and I took a trip to Leeds General Hospital to meet Professor Simon Kay and the team who had performed the first single hand transplant in the UK. I knew I was feeling negative about it, but felt I owed it to Professor Hart to keep an open mind. I have to admit that on the way home that day I was swayed a bit.

I was surprised to hear that they weren't sure I would be acceptable to them, so clearly there was no decision for me to make yet until I knew what their decision was.

We went back in April for physiological examinations, which was unfortunate timing as I was feeling particularly emotional that week. I had a new specialist nurse in Glasgow and a new psychologist, too, added to this new psychologist in Leeds. And it meant that I had to start at the beginning, telling them all my story separately.

It had become expected that I would fill up talking about Rory at any time, and clearly his welfare and the relationship with his dad was delicate and raw. I soaked a few hankies that day in Leeds with Dr Maggie Bellow, and felt certain that meant that I wouldn't pass their tests. I also had discussions with the physiotherapists and drug specialists, where I learned that immune suppressants were only one part of the deal. There would also be a year of steroids, which were sure to puff me up like a balloon and make me feel crap.

Additionally, the increased risks of cancers were not to be taken lightly, and I was warned that a suntan was a thing of the past, as skin cancer is one of the more likely possibilities when your immune system is reduced. Professor Kay helpfully suggested that there were some creams available that tanned your skin artificially. No shit! With a pale blue Glasgow tan like mine, those creams had been a constant for years, but thanks, Prof. Bless him!

I had to do a series of IQ tests, too, to prove that I was of sound mind (!!) to make this huge decision. Puzzles are my thing, so it felt like a bit of a playday for me to be doing word associations, solving problems, etc. But I was doing them for hours while my poor dad sat outside in the car!

In May, I was told by the team that I was a good candidate for transplant, by which time Dad, David and I were convinced that it would be great for me to be 'part fixed'. Mum and my other brother, Scott, were not convinced, and were very worried about the health risks which had been pointed out by medical friends.

Matching me to a potential donor appeared to be the biggest, most important hurdle. After 25 blood transfusions and giving birth to a child, my body had been exposed to substantially more antibodies than most people have, and a donor would have to NOT have those same antibodies. That wouldn't be easy to find.

One more visit to Leeds was necessary. The team were holding a meeting with all the relevant medical staff to discuss my possible operation, and they asked if I'd like to go. So off Dad and I went again for the eight-hour round trip to Leeds, listening to talking books all the way. I knew some of the staff from Glasgow Royal were attending, too, as they would be very involved in the preparation for the operation and in my rehabilitation.

Jennifer Lang was my main hand physio after my amputations, and I was delighted to know that she'd be in charge of getting my new hands working. She was tough, hurt me a lot and pushed me hard, but I knew that's what would bring the best results.

The meeting in Leeds was a shocker, though. It was held in a mini-amphitheatre with approx. 25 to 30 staff present. I assumed there were other operations to be discussed as well as mine, but embarrassingly, they were all there to discuss me! The detail they went into about the procedures and methods to be used was way above my head, but you could tell there wasn't a single detail I could have thought of that they hadn't already, and I was a bit overwhelmed about it all.

There were organ donation nurses, whose job it would be to convince families to donate organs from lost loved ones. That was very grounding, and it always stops me in my tracks to think that someone has to die to give me this chance of new hands. How awful is that?

I was spoken to by the hospital PR person, who went into detail about how to handle the huge press interest that would be generated by being a double hand transplant. He suggested I needed to watch what I was putting in my bins, check all online social media in my name, and clear out any photos or information that was less than flattering. Really?

You only have to look at my Facebook page to see that most photos of me are unflattering, but I don't think I've much to hide and I'm certainly not going to contact all my 'friends' and ask them to remove them all. I'd sound like such a diva. I can't believe there would be that much interest in me for long, though, so I didn't do anything much!

Also there was Mark Cahill, who was the first — and at that time, only — person in the UK to have undergone a hand transplant; he was asked to come and talk to me, and answer any questions I had. Mark told me what a hard time he'd had with the press, though, and it was an eye-opener. From the very distant acquaintance that had now promoted himself to best friend and given quotes to the media, to the persistent and constant press presence outside his door. Wow!

We agreed between us that the best course of action might be for me to tell no one about the operation for a while and announce it when we chose to, which would spare my parents, Rory, and his dad, etc. I knew it would bounce off me, but not them.

When it *was* announced, they were right; it went mad. I was on my way to stay with friends in Seattle who had worried a lot about me, and I felt I was due the trip to see them in my second chance at life. (Any excuse for the fabulous trip!). By the time I'd stopped in Philadelphia, I had received loads of messages and had to record a response in the airport.

Rory, Kate, Huck and I had built in a cheeky wee trip when we knew we were going to be in Philadelphia, and we set off in a taxi to the enormous set of steps made famous in the *Rocky* movie, to attempt to run up them!

Kate filmed, while the kids and I built ourselves up for the challenge. I even wrapped a towel around my neck for effect! We did it, and it felt great to be doing something I had never thought I would ever do again and that others thought I'd never do again, too. We had a lot of laughs doing it, and any positive feeling like that is so much better than any negative feelings if you're not pushing yourself. The video shows Huck really supporting me, and we did the big Rocky punch at the top. Rory was totally blasé about it and couldn't even manage a hug! He certainly keeps my feet on the ground.

On my return, we agreed to a start date for the donor search as 1st September, 2014, and I packed my bag ready for the emergency call, which meant I was to be on call 24/7. In the year following that, I had five false alarms for a suitable match. That meant receiving the initial call from Professor Kay, or his registrar Anna Bernard, that a potential donor had been found.

The next stage was for the donor's family to agree, and one fell down then as the family weren't happy about the press attention. If the family agreed, Professor Kay or Anna had to personally see the donor's hands, which meant that a one-hour radius of Leeds was all that could be included. On one occasion they decided the hands weren't a good enough visual match; another time the donor's hands weren't viable.

The next step involves a series of very specific blood matches, checking those antibodies. Twice we got to the very last stages, but six or seven hours later, I was told that they weren't a good enough match.

I was surprised to feel quite relieved most of those times when the transplant fell through, but I think that's just because I knew that post-op was going to be so difficult for me and for so long. Then the disappointment would set in.

I began to feel like this affected everything in my life — my diary and any appointments had to be set 'subject to operation'; my holidays had to be chosen close to home so that I was within reach of Leeds; and if I chose to go abroad, I had to take myself off the waiting list. Obviously, I didn't want to do that more than necessary.

Not telling anyone when the call came in was quite a challenge. Each time was different and threw up a new set of considerations. One time Rory was at his dad's and was due to return the following morning, when I would be gone. We debated about not telling him so that he didn't tell anyone else, but how could you do that? I didn't want him lied to, so when that one failed, I sat him down and tried to explain why it would be good for him to keep it a secret from his school pals.

We had a list of friends and family who would be told, and that task fell to Kate, the gatekeeper! Depending on who I was with at the time would decide who would know, though, so every instance was different.

I decided to do as the Leeds PR team had suggested and I put out a Facebook post asking, in the nicest possible way, for discretion if and when it happened. I had to ask friends not to post good luck messages or well wishes out in the open forum, and I asked them to consider the donor's family and my family, to save them from press intrusion. What a diva, right enough! I was quite embarrassed but knew it was necessary.

I got a lovely message complimenting me on my consideration from a mum who had donated her daughter's organs on her death. I felt a fraud, as I was only doing as I was told to do, but it led to a meeting where I got to ask how it felt from the other side. I think that helped me to understand what an awful decision organ donation is for any family.

I have always carried a Donor Card, but waiting for a transplant made me realise how few do. Many people say to me that they've never got around to it, or were too superstitious to complete the form. Someone also pointed out how many deaths lead to cremation now, and it's quite thought-provoking to think what a waste that is.

I always felt hands were functional and useful but, let's face it, not life-threatening. Just imagine your child is waiting on a vital organ to save their life and how many transplant organs are lost to cremation because of that difficult question. Soft opt-out organ donation has to be the way forward, where the default will be that everyone is an organ donor, unless they've opted not to. That way you get the choice, but apathy isn't an option.

In the meantime, I'd urge everyone to make the choice beforehand and spare your family having to be in that dreadful position. Ashley, the charity's PR guru at the time, and I agreed to do a stunt where a medical illustrator painted all transplantable organs (including hands) onto my naked body, and I was then photographed professionally. Ashley left for London and, with the help of a guerilla marketing team, my picture was projected onto key landmark buildings in London in 'Organ Donation Week'. That got the message across, I think!

***

Colin, Dad

When it was first mooted that Corinne was an ideal candidate for the double hand transplant, I am sure that her surgeon Professor Andrew Hart recognised her strength of character, something she would require to have to carry her through this difficult period.

As a family, we weighed up all the pros and cons of this operation — and, believe me, there are a lot of cons but one very big pro. Corinne took very little time to decide that she wanted to undertake this venture, even though she would be back to being unable to do anything for herself — including driving — for some months. Fortunately, Corinne bought the house next door to us a few years ago, to look after us in our old age! So Doreen and I are pleased that we will be on hand to look after her, and do whatever is required.

Professor Hart set up a meeting in Leeds with one of his colleagues, Professor Simon Kay, who carried out the UK's first single hand transplant. Corinne and I drove down to

Leeds for what was to be the first of many such meetings. During this meeting, Professor Kay praised his colleague for his foresight in leaving Corinne's 'hands' in such a way as to be suitable to receive donor hands. This made us realise that Professor Hart had realised during the amputations that he could save parts of 'hands', i.e. knuckles, bones, ligaments, nerves, etc, should transplants become a reality.

Meeting Mark Cahill — the first hand transplant patient — gave both of us a great deal of encouragement and hope, as although it was about 14 months since his operation, he had already recovered his sense of touch. I know this is very important to Corinne, as what she misses most is not being able to hold Rory's hand and run her fingers through his hair. Just writing this brings back that huge lump to my throat and tears to my eyes.

The biggest concern that I had was that Corinne would be on anti-rejection drugs for the rest of her life.

On our next visit to Leeds, about a month later, Corinne and I were surprised to find a room full of medics, including Professor Hart and a team from the Royal Infirmary in Glasgow. All of those present — surgeons, doctors, nurses, physios, occupational therapists — would be involved in Corinne's operation and the aftermath.

Soon after was another trip to Leeds, this time for Corinne to have a test to assess that she had the correct mental attitude to cope with what would be a very traumatic period in her life. She passed! Although I never had any doubt that she would.

The ball was now well and truly in motion, and Professor Kay told us that, unlike organs which can be harvested *anywhere in the UK, kept alive and transported to the hospital where they would be transplanted, donor hands are totally different. When a potential donor is found, they have to stay on life support, and blood group and tissue samples have to match Corinne's. Professor Kay would then go to the donor's hospital to do a physical comparison. This put limits on the potential catchment area as realistically being within one-and-a-half hours of Leeds; only seven hospitals fall into this category.*

Corinne was told to go home and pack a case, as she was now on a four-hour standby. This said, Professor Kay said not to build her hopes up too high as it could take a year, possibly two, to find a suitable donor. To date, Corinne has been on standby eight times.

Corinne has lived up to her promise to me to not be disabled, as she works out in the gym and swims twice a week. When she agreed to undertake a 10km assault course to raise funds for the Finding Your Feet charity, at that stage in her recovery I thought it would be too much for her, but knew that there was no point in arguing with her. The obstacles consisted of crawling under cargo nets, climbing over netted A-frames, walking over logs across ditches, etc. The only answer was for me to do it with her, so that we could pull out if I thought it was getting too much for her.

She, of course, completed the course, which necessitated having her 'spare legs' inserted into a pair of chest-high fisherman's waders, which I carried in a rucksack. At each of the three river crossings she had to sit down on the muddy river bank — it was very wet that day — take off her prosthetic legs, put on the spare ones (complete with waders), make the

river crossing, and then repeat the change of legs process on the other bank. All these delays meant that Corinne was never going to win, but so what? Just to finish was a great achievement.

Next up was a Finding Your Feet event, cycling 11 miles around Millport with about 50 families – some with children who had also lost limbs. Mums and dads pulled most of these children around on bike trailers, but one child, Charlotte — a six-year-old quadruple amputee — wanted to cycle herself on a specially adapted trike which the charity had hired for her. She only managed about a mile, but what a tremendous spirit this child had. She could perform 'handstands' on her elbows, and played football on her knees with Rory.

Finding Your Feet now organises an annual 92km (58 mile) cycle around a very hilly Isle of Arran, and in its second year Corinne said she wanted to participate. So she found two riders who were willing to do the cycle in a relay. With her willpower and sheer determination, she managed the 20 miles up the west coast from Blackwaterfoot to Lochranza, only falling off twice, ripping her Lycra trousers and her backside in the process. As her caring father, I offered to kiss it better – she declined, and got back on her bike.

Corinne always had a notion to learn to fly, so she found a flying school that was agreeable to let her fly – no hands and feet, and she's flying a plane. The mind boggles!

The father of a family friend, Jim Campbell, wanted to climb Scotland's highest mountain, Ben Nevis (4,409 feet), to raise money for Finding Your Feet on his 80th birthday. He had previously climbed Ben Nevis on his 70th and 75th birthdays. About ten of his family agreed to support him on his challenge, and they asked Corinne to accompany them. Before her illness, Corinne was very much into hillwalking, having climbed Ben Lomond and trekked in the Himalayas. So she didn't take much persuading.

She was, however, concerned that if she couldn't complete the climb and had to turn back, one of the party would be obliged to turn back, too. Therefore, Father was roped in again! Six hours up and four hours down, with a two-and-a-half-hour drive before and after; a totally knackering day for both of us.

On the long drive home, I was kept awake — fortunately, I was driving — by the enormity of her achievement. The first female quadruple amputee to climb Britain's highest mountain. I was a very proud father. However, on arriving home, neither of us could get out of the car!

Through Jim Campbell's efforts on this climb and other fundraising activities, he raised so much in sponsorship that he was the charity's most successful single fundraiser that year. And his efforts were recognised at the charity's annual fundraising dinner.

Another Finding Your Feet fundraising event was to abseil 140 feet down one of Glasgow's highest buildings and yes, you've guessed it, Corinne had to do it.

I have asked her to scale down her ambitious challenges as I, at 72 years of age, have to do them with her. Thankfully, I did manage to escape the abseil, as I was in America at the time.

In recognition of her achievements, Corinne was a finalist in the Mountain Warehouse Charity Challenge of the Year

Awards, and then won a Scottish Sunday Mail Great Scot Award (with a personal video tribute from Katie Piper). At the Commonwealth Games in Glasgow, she was invited to carry the baton in the Queen's baton relay, and in December 2016 she was invited to meet Prime Minister David Cameron at Downing Street. In February 2016 Corinne was awarded the Freedom of Renfrewshire, and in June, a Point of Light award from the Prime Minister. I only seem to get to do the daft things!

Corinne's achievements, her cheery personality, and her unstinting attitude in supporting others who have suffered a life-changing trauma, make me so very proud to be her dad. But she'll always be my little girl.

Transplant donation poster in Covent Garden

Cycling with Keeley
© John Linton

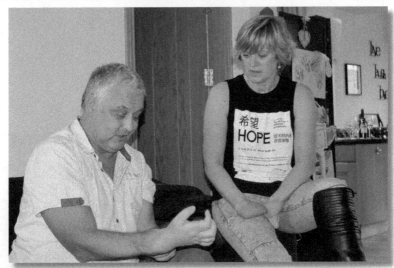

Mark Cahill, recipient of Britains first double hand transplant

Freedom of Renfrewshire

Receiving an Honorary Doctorate from the
University of the West of Scotland.

CHAPTER 8
WAITING

Waiting for hands; after 22 months, I'm getting frustrated at the lack of progress. I haven't had a false alarm for months, and I never hear anything in between. I'm sure they're discussing this constantly in Leeds, but I don't hear a word, which leaves me to think nothing's happening and I feel isolated and forgotten.

I was their star patient. I was to be their first ever double hand transplant. Now others have been given the chance, and rightly so, but I'm now just a number and only one of a few competing for the very scarce hands donated by grieving families in the Leeds area. How dreadful I feel being impatient and frustrated when someone needs to die to give me their hands! But how long can I bear to have my life on hold?

I have to step down from transplant if I go abroad, so naturally I don't want to go away much, but that conflicts with my 'second chance' rule of living every moment. I turn down opportunities and select my destinations close to home, just in case. I pre-empt every meeting or booking with 'operation dependent' and keep all my life in order in the event of 'that call'.

Even my washing basket has to be kept low, just in case. Heaven forbid, someone would have to do my laundry for me, or iron Rory's karate kit while I'm in hospital!

I'm excited but very nervous of the after-op life, which will be torture for me for several months. Six months of no driving, complete dependence, arse wiping, cooking, cleaning, uselessness. Actually, as I'm typing, maybe it doesn't sound sooo bad!

For someone so fiercely independent and having fought back to a good, full and positive life, I am going to struggle to voluntarily give it all up whilst not being 'sick' enough to need bed rest. It might take two years of physio, too.

Every false alarm I've had brings mixed emotions. To help you understand, it works like this.

A potential donor is found from some poor souls facing the loss of their loved one, who must be already registered on the donor list for other organs. No family is even asked to donate if they are not registered. Human rights, apparently, prevents that very open question where family have the option to say no.

The family then need to agree to switch off the life support machine at some point, and may face an extra question of possible tissue and hand donation. That means people who die in their sleep, or at the scene of an accident, for example, are excluded from donation.

The surgeons have to view any potential donor hands, so that's the next step, meaning they can't look too far from Leeds. After harvesting hands, the lack of circulation in hands quickly causes them to decay, so transporting them long distances is out, too.

The surgeons have to look for a visual match, as well as blood/tissue match, adding another dimension to hearts, lungs, etc, where the look, donor's sex, size, etc, matters less.

Professor Kay's registrar Anna Barnard turned out to be exactly the right size and colour for me, but she wouldn't give me her hands! What does a surgeon need her hands for? It's 'handy', though, in finding a visual match when she is attending with model hands to compare!

The next step, if the donor hands are acceptable, is to ask the family to donate them. As this is a fairly new pioneering procedure, not many are keen to agree. Should they do so, a series of blood tests needs to happen to see if the hands would be an acceptable blood match.

As a layman, my understanding is that we all have a set of antibodies in us. A mother has been exposed to her child's antibodies and, in my case, having had 25 blood transfusions — then 25 extra sets of antibodies — my body has had to cope with two extra sets of antibodies. The donor needs to have none of those antibodies, or rejection is a risk. As such, it seems like we're looking for a needle in a haystack.

The furthest of the false alarms I've had reached the

very last stage of blood testing. At that point, seven hours on from the first alert, Professor Hart had arranged to have a helicopter at Glasgow Airport; I had lists of instructions for Rory's diary events at school and clubs; and I'd updated the girls at Finding Your Feet so as not to leave anyone in the lurch. Sadly, it didn't happen, and the tests fell at the final hurdle. I was surprised to feel relief as well as disappointment.

I hate procrastination and talking about things then not doing them, so my frustration was as much about the waste of time spent organising. Both Professors were gutted for me — and I'm sure for them, too — but they assured me it will happen eventually.

Why me?

When I first began to recover, I was often told, 'It's okay to think, why me?' But after the first time I thought it, I questioned, well, if not me… who? Rory? My parents? My brothers? That really scared me, and I decided to be glad it was me and not them, nor my friends, nor someone who wasn't as strong and couldn't deal with it. That's not to say I don't wish it hadn't happened to me, but if it was them or me, I'd pick me!

Like most people do, I thought I wouldn't be able to do much. On the contrary, I manage most things, but they take longer or I have to work out other ways of doing them. I use my teeth far too much, and have had to have a few repairs after using them to pull, open, or hold something; once I broke a tooth pulling out a knot in Rory's shoelaces!

My forearms and elbows come in handy, for example, when I went tree trekking with the kids on an adventure holiday. The guides felt I would manage to go around the circuit, 40 feet up. They would help me, and I would be harnessed, so what could possibly go wrong? I used my elbows and forearms to grip the ropes as I held on, and made my way around moving steps, bridges and platforms, ending in a zip slide. By the end, my bare arms were badly scraped, burnt, and bruised, from my shoulders to my wrists, but I was delirious at gaining my certificate.

My determination and pride, however, gets me into many sticky wickets, as I refuse to say 'no' or 'I can't'. Recently, I was trying rock climbing with others affected by limb-loss, in an activity organised by Finding Your Feet. Ryan (10) and Daniel (7) each have a missing hand from birth; Keeley (7) lost a leg at birth; and adult Becca lost hers as a baby.

The determination shown by all of us impressed those watching, but I got two-thirds of the way up and had a panic attack from fear of heights. My grip wasn't good, as my 'mitts' didn't slot into many hand-holds very well, my thighs were shaking from effort, and my upper arms and shoulders were aching from being so tense and clinging onto anything I could.

The spectators were on a platform at my level and they were taking pictures. I hate to fail, so I was feeling the pressure and wishing I could just give up. I looked up and counted how many steps I'd have to take, then went for it. There's no way I wanted to have to repeat all that I'd done. Dig deep and grit your teeth, and that gets you a bit further.

As if that wasn't enough, though, my wee friend Keeley was determined I had to crawl through the kids' tunnel with her. She wouldn't go without me, and needed a punty near the start. Her parents were in the comfortable spectator area, so I felt I had to go with her.

It involved a shallow start, where I had to squeeze my legs in first before helping Keeley up, climbing up behind her into another tunnel four feet up, without much to grip onto at either foot level or hand level. After a couple of nervous shaky positions, I got up and crawled into the next section, only to find I had to drop down the same on the other side.

I decided to come down on my stomach, which meant I couldn't see down — and I was honestly panicking. Keeley was shouting, 'Come on, Corinne' over and over again, and I was threatening to murder her! After crawling out on all fours, I realised I had torn my leggings in several places on both knees, and permanently scratched my bespoke Finding Your Feet legs. Keeley was in big trouble! She obviously thinks we can both do anything.

***

When I was first home and not so well, my friends would come round and offer to do things, but I was very proud and wanted them to see 'capable me', so I'd say I didn't need anything and they'd just start cleaning or something. We agreed that I would keep a wee pile of things needing done, and when they came round, they could pick one to do for me. So light bulbs, sewing, jewellery, etc, have all been waiting for them on arrival, before or with a good blether and a glass of wine. I actually 'can't' do earrings. I hate saying can't, but it's just not possible and I need someone to do them for me. My friends love these easy things! They also tuck my trousers into my boots or pull up a zip for me!

People are often nervous of asking if they can help when they see me tackling something difficult. For example, a sachet of sugar, or sauce, or a biscuit wrapper, but I'm embarrassed that when they do offer, I've invariably tried and covered said item in saliva! I try to laugh at these situations and make people feel more comfortable. I don't have a problem with them offering, and I don't have a problem with asking when I need help, either, like getting the coin out of my gym locker. I just ask anyone passing and they're always keen to help.

I've met people who get annoyed at someone offering to help. They say they manage fine when no-one is there to offer, so why would they need help now? I do understand that, but I also see someone being kind and I wouldn't want to stop them offering the next time. The next person might really need their help.

Some disabled people, I notice, carry a real chip on their shoulder. They seem to look for people who've insulted them by offering to help, or offended them by holding a door open, or parked in a disabled space when they have no disability. Okay, that last one is wrong and you shouldn't do it, but I'm far too busy to go looking around car parks to spot it. Maybe I don't see the rudeness or the disapproval as I wear rose-tinted glasses, or maybe they're looking too hard for the insult due to their inferiority complexes. Probably both, I suspect. I think it's easier — and better — to give people the benefit of the doubt.

***

Nicola Booth, Finding Your Feet friend

It's almost a cliché now, but the first time I met Cor, I didn't immediately notice that she had no hands. And I've lost count of the number of people who this happens with. She's so smiley, friendly, and engaging that you immediately get caught up in the warm welcome and easy conversation; and it's only when you take the time to remember who you're talking to, that you realise she has no hands or feet.

Everyone that meets Cor can't help but be overwhelmed by the enormity of what she has gone through and how incredible she has become as a result. This means that she's regularly put on a pedestal and adored. I adore her, too. How could I not? However, I also have the privilege of being her friend which means I see a side of her that not everyone does. And I don't think I've ever laughed so much as I have since meeting Cor and joining the Finding Your Feet team.

Unfortunately for Cor, most of the amusement she gener-ates is at her own expense. A perfect example is while the

FYF team were taking on a 5k obstacle course with her, just 18 months after her amputations. The stories we tell are of how Cor marched ahead up the hills while shouting at us to keep up. The stories that don't make the press are the ones like when she tripped and fell flat on her face in the mud. After an initial quick check to make sure she was okay, the hysterics ensued, while poor Cor was left lying in the mud.

At another event where Cor was supposed to be working, we (easily) persuaded her to have a go on the 120ft water slide, without giving enough thought to the damage she might do her legs as she tumbled down a slippery wet plastic sheet edged with heavy tyres. Again, a quick check that she was ok, and then the laughing started, probably before we helped her up.

She's up for anything, which makes her not only great fun to work with, but a fantastic person to front Finding Your Feet. There's so much scope for getting her to take on challenges most people would never even consider, even those with all four limbs intact.

***

Ashley Reid, Finding Your Feet friend

My youngest, Monty, has met Corinne on many occasions, although it took until recently for him to notice she has no hands. I like that. Kids don't notice, don't care.

'I need a juice,' Monty barks at Corinne, as he surveys her kitchen with a look one can only describe as akin to

disdain. Corinne's kitchen is, in fact, rather lovely. My child is despicable.

Corinne obliges his demands, in spite of my half-hearted protestations, and fetches Monty a familiar brand of fruit smoothie from her well-stocked fridge. In typical maternal-style, I urge Monty to express the obligatory gratitude; ignoring me, Corinne raises her right arm and says, 'Gimme a high five, Monty.'

Now, giving a 'high-five' when you in fact have not five, but indeed no digits at all, is nothing short of impossible. And while Corinne and I may not have appreciated this fact, three-year-old Monty appraises the sight before him instantly, not without a level of intrigue and resourcefulness that, it turned out, made me somewhat proud.

'Why don't you have any hands?' Monty asks indignantly.

Used to the situation, such questions and reactions phase neither myself nor Corinne, and I quickly start to remind Monty that Mummy works with Corinne because her hands got sick...

I needn't have bothered. 'Fist pump?' asks Monty, his face now beaming with glee as he raises his clenched fist and purposefully bashes his soft tiny hand against Corinne's stump.

Kids rock.

***

'Why does Corinne have no legs?'

Jennie has asked this question a lot. I tend to explain it by saying that Corinne got very sick, in a way that not many people get sick — 'So don't worry, Jennie, it's not going to

happen to you.' — but that her hands and feet were so very sick the doctors needed to take them away. My job is to help Corinne get new hands (thankfully the question of where her new hands come from has not, at time of writing, been asked), and to help her and lots of others like her to achieve all the things they want to, through Finding Your Feet.

For three years, I co-ran the charity with Corinne — trying to maintain some kind of direction and structure. Our modest team, of which I am enormously proud, was ever-expanding. Corinne Hutton has become a super hero.

CHAPTER 9
WITH A LOT OF HELP FROM MY FRIENDS

I'd been out of hospital just a few days when the girls suggested a wee trip to celebrate. Mor said she had looked into the trains, how to get my wheelchair on and off at our stations, and spoken to Scotrail about ramps. She had worked out how to get to and from the restaurant from the station, and she had spoken to our special haunt, Scotts of Troon, about access and table position. She had it all worked out to make sure I could do what used to make me happy.

We got on the train at Johnstone, as Lochwinnoch Station has a flight of steps which is useless for wheelchairs. The train attendant couldn't have been more helpful and everything went quite smoothly. It was a 'first' in terms of really getting out and doing what I would have done previously. Safely on the train, the champagne was opened and a photo taken to mark the occasion — both long-standing traditions.

The meal went without incident, although there was a real learning curve to find out what I could order that

I could actually get into my mouth and what I could manage to drink without losing control of my emotions.

The train journey home wasn't so smooth. The taxi driver at the restaurant wasn't pleased at having to remove his ramp to allow access for my wheelchair. He probably wasn't exactly rude, but he was irritated and I was very sensitive to these reactions. At Troon Station, the train arrived but there was no attendant and no ramp. After a few moments' hold-up, an attendant was found and I was wheeled onto the train to what I thought would be irritated passengers already on board.

None of these were dreadfully bad events under normal circumstances, but at that stage I was self-conscious, embarrassed, and probably tired, with alcohol in me. The taxi ride home from the station took forever and I couldn't wait to get in the door, knowing I was ready to bawl my eyes out. And that's exactly what I did.

I'm now very aware of my emotions when I'm tired, and particularly under the influence of a few champers. But then, I was probably always emotional like that. A night's sleep is a great healer, though, and I'm usually much more positive in the morning.

I received a photo message the next day, recording the train journey with all my friends who loved me and were glad I hadn't died. Under closer inspection of the photo, though, I discovered I was sitting right underneath a sign — a disabled sign! — and wondered if they had orchestrated that or if it had been an accident. Oh yes, bessi mates!

***

Arlene & Irene, friends

The Howwood Inn was where we first met Cor, when she owned it with Kate and Davy. Loving her sense of humour and zest for life, we became friends and soon were roped into fundraising for her and Mor, as part of their Great Wall of China Charity Bike Ride. After several girlie nights out and weekends away — Amsterdam, Dublin, Ardwell, to name but a few — we were part of the gang.

Cor's enthusiasm spilled over, and before long we had signed up to walk the Himalayas in aid of Maggie's Cancer Care, along with Cor's dad, Colin. A particular memory is on the final ascent in the Himalayas, the group set off early morning but us three were singing and carrying on —- it was like a scene from **The Sound of Music** *— only to be told by the trek doctor to 'calm down and save our energy'. The doc was blaming the altitude but we were just 'living the moment' of being in the Himalayas; not many people can say that!*

Charity challenges became 'our thing' – Maggie's Monster Bike Hike, the Mighty Deerstalker, and the Kiltwalk. At six months pregnant, Cor was determined to take part in the first leg of the Monster Bike Hike, a 33-mile cycle over rough terrain, much to the annoyance of some of the team.

In April 2013, we completed the Glasgow Kiltwalk. Little did we know that this was to be Cor's last challenge before her biggest: staying alive.

It was a beautiful day in June, and Irene and I were meeting friends for a liquid lunch in Merchant City. Whilst

*sitting in the sun, we were oblivious that Cor was uncon-
scious, fighting for life. Morning followed a sleepless night,
waiting for the good news that she was going to be okay. As
hours passed into days, time stood still until we were eventually told she was 'out of immediate danger'.*

*When we eventually got to visit Corinne, we had prepped
each other on what we should say and how we should act,
i.e. act and speak normal, and not be afraid to laugh. This
was made easy when I leaned over the bed and knocked
her catheter off its hook and flooded the place, much to the
bemusement of the nursing staff. At least we succeeded in
making Cor chuckle.*

*Her determination to lead her life as we do is actually
what makes her stand out from the crowd... along with her
sense of humour and her love for Rory. Disability — what
disability?*

Arlene

***

*Corinne has the same competitive nature
as Arlene and I have, and our many challenges have given us great laughs along
the way.*

*The final challenge was six weeks before
her illness, the Glasgow Kiltwalk – 26 miles from Hampden
Park to Loch Lomond. We completed the walk, celebrated
with champagne, and talked about our next challenge... But
it was never to be; well, not for a long time after. Never in
a million years did we imagine what was going to happen
six weeks later.*

On the afternoon of that awful day, Arlene and I were out lunching and drinking wine, sitting in the sunshine with a group of friends. By the time we got home, we had text messages to say that Cor was in renal failure. It was hard to comprehend — things like that don't happen to people like Cor. She was dying and there was nothing we could do. A mixed bag of emotions — helpless, sad, lack of understanding how it happened.

The ECMO machine kept her alive but not without huge consequences. When Cor was transferred back to Paisley RAH, we got to see her and she put on a brave face as if everything was fine. Much as we wanted to say everything was going to be okay, the blackness of her hands and feet made this very difficult. She was moved to the Glasgow Royal Infirmary, and the shock of her amputations was unimaginable.

Three years down the line, we can say that sometimes we forget Cor has a disability, and I think that's what a lot of people think when they first meet her. She has overcome something that the majority of us couldn't (I know I couldn't), and she has set out to ensure that others in her position shall have a life and can overcome anything. She's succeeded in this, and for that it is an absolute pleasure for us to be friends with Cor.

Irene

"Great friends?!"

CHAPTER 10
BEST FOOT FORWARD

After the initial ball-rolling to raise money for 'poor Corinne', the attention changed from me to other amputees, or those with limb difference.

Finding Your Feet currently arranges sporting activities like climbing, abseiling, cycling, swimming, skiing, yoga, and movement therapy to help posture, health and attitude, as well as confidence and self-esteem. Many people suffer amputation because of lifestyle, and they tend not be sporty or energetic. For them, our sporting events are not really of interest, so we felt the need to arrange less active, more tame events like coffee mornings (ampuTEAS!), day trips, crafting, beauty sessions, etc, and the plan is to create a FYF band and an art club too.

A very high percentage of amputees don't receive prosthetics for very good reasons, like health prognosis, activity level, age and attitude, and I was shocked to find that they only receive a wheelchair and are then sent home. My positivity was a result of being kept busy, attending physio and prosthetic appointments, and getting out and about. My fear for those less lucky was that they would suffer from negativity; apparently the mortality rate is actually far younger in this case, thereby concluding that lack of hope and less activity reduces the will to live. How horrible! We must help.

I set out to arrange for foot soldiers to go to see people in their homes, in cases where they were unable to come to our events. It seemed essential to search out networks in their areas that would allow them to get out to clubs, meet peers, and find some positivity in their new lives. So that what's we did. Emotional support wasn't something I had really seen as being important; I guess that's because I just had it. It wasn't offered or discussed. I just happen to be very lucky to have a great network of friends and family.

Now I see it as being the key to survival and finding your feet when your world crashes down on you. Not a cotton-woolly thing, either, but more a 'laugh at yourself' kind of thing. 'Laughter, the best medicine' was certainly true in my case, and it's what we try to offer.

In my case, I wouldn't have wanted 'help', but people who really understood would have been gratefully appreciated.

The dream is to have several of these networks up and down the length of the UK, where amputees or those who lose limb function can 'find their feet' and get back to the life they lost, or perhaps the best life they can live in their new situation. In fact, we now have a Dundee group who meet and have their own groups of yoga, swimming and AmpuTEAS.

I have many new friends all over the country, and in time wouldn't it be good if some of them went to visit new amputees in hospital and offered support and friendship at their lowest point? The extra benefit is that it makes *us* feel useful and important, and to feel that you've made a difference to just one person is hugely rewarding. From being useless and helpless in hospital, to doing a job that really matters to someone. Made to measure!

Finding Your Feet, the charity we set up, raised over £200,000 in its first year-and-a-half and three years on is helping many amputees, a stroke victim, limb-affected kids and their parents to find THEIR feet and be all they can be. That's not a bad start, but I'm well aware of how lucky I am to have the support network I have. I want to offer that help to anyone else who needs a 'leg up' or a 'helping hand'.

We are still having good fun with a publicity campaign that started by accident by a rather handsome benefactor. Gerard Butler, the dreamy Scots actor heard about my hand transplant and wanted to 'lend a hand' and sent us a papyrus sheet with his huge hand prints on it. This started a wave of offers from sports stars, movie stars, politicians, TV presenters, past and present and we now have a gallery of about 70 that will one day be sold for funds to support our 'troopers'. Mel Gibson, Andy Murray, Nicola Sturgeon all adding weight to the campaign.

A lot of words like 'can't' can now be replaced with 'yes I can'. And if I can, I'll show others how to.

At Finding Your Feet, we set about defying normal and decided we would encourage our troopers to embrace 'unique' or 'interestingly different'. Our campaign '50 shades of normal' was designed to ridicule everyone's need to be 'normal'.

Finding Your Feet's role is to be that support network that I was so lucky to have, to pass on everything we've learned, and to help people find their feet, either physically or metaphorically.

My feeling, from experience, is that if we're left to our own company too much, we over-think and dwell on our problems, and it leads to negativity and depressive feelings. I do struggle with things and many take me longer and more effort than most, but this is life for me now and it's preferable to being a recluse and feeling sorry for myself. Sometimes I have down times. Sometimes I struggle to get myself out of them. Ultimately, though, I don't want to feel like that. I want to laugh and to live, and so I CHOOSE to be happy. It's not automatic; it needs effort and a desire to get to that happy place.

It provides me with good experience for my job, though, as frequently I come across people who aren't able to pick themselves up and who retreat into isolation rather than being seen to be down in public. I get that feeling, I really do, but I also hate it and I assume they do, too.

My answer is to do things that make you laugh, and spend time with people who can help you do that. LAUGHTER, THE BEST MEDICINE. Undoubtedly, it is the most underrated therapy and much cheaper than most, too! Even if it only gives you an hour or two of relief, it's worth it. If you can possibly do something that you thought you couldn't do — or even better, something that other people didn't think you could do — the buzz from that is great therapy.

Neither feeling sorry for myself nor laughing will bring back my hands or legs, unfortunately. But it's about rescuing a decent life for yourself and getting back to what was important to you.

It's about looking forward, and not dwelling on the past. I didn't die, and I'm going to make sure I LIVE.

With Finding Your Feet, I will visit an amputee — or potential amputee — as early as I'm invited to. I often wonder what I think I'm doing there, or why I think I can make a difference, but actually all I'm trying to do is give them some hope. They won't be necessarily interested in the same things as me, but being able to show them that it can be done might just give them something positive to take away.

Of course, some probably want to punch me for being too bloody cheerful! Davy always quotes: 'Not every day's a good day, but there is good in every day.' If you can just find that wee glimmer of light in every day, however small, it's a positive to cling onto.

 Later, when they are ready — and usually when rehabilitation ends — there's a gap where they're not out at physio any more, their hospital appointments have slowed down, and they're not meeting other patients any more. Yet they are not yet ready and capable of getting back to their lives, so that's where most people hit a wall.

I was always delighted and excited with the smallest little achievement for months and months, but then you start to plateau where the 'firsts' are not so common and the buzz slows down. That's where I fell. And from a great height, too! Just when everyone thought I was over the worst and in control; when the worst of the learning curve was behind me; when I thought I was able to do everything and as much of it as I wanted to. Suddenly I realised that I couldn't. I pushed myself too hard and put myself under too much pressure, and I broke.

I was quite quick to understand what was going on and sought help from the psychologist Paul at West-MARC. I'd met him several times, when he helped us in the charity, and I had been quick to tell him that I didn't need help. I explained to him that no-one could kick their own butt better than me, and I didn't allow myself to get down for long.

All of that was still true. But temporarily, I needed put back on track. So I spent a few sessions with him and was staggered at how often I said that I felt guilty. Guilty that I'd put everyone through this. Guilty that I wasn't able to be everything I had once been to everybody. A bad mum. A useless businesswoman. Failed marriages. You name it; I felt a lot of guilt. I also felt really inferior and useless. Both my brothers were successful. My mum and dad were successful. But I was dependent physically and financially. I was taking from my parents, and I felt guilty and worthless for that.

All this guilt came out in my discussions with Paul, but he reasoned with me, too. He made me realise how guilty they would be feeling. Useless, too, perhaps. He made me choose what was more important in my life (Rory) and to prioritise that. If I wanted to be there for Rory, that was important. If I felt obliged to do a talk or a meeting, that might not be so important and I needed to be able to say 'no'. People would understand, but I needed to control my time better and in line with what was important to me.

I got good at that for a while, but I'm still guilty of saying 'yes' to too much, and for not wanting to let anyone down. I learned that mindfulness and self-preservation are very important if we want to be of use to others, but I forget to apply it a lot!

I have always 'communicated fluently', since my school report cards, so it is no surprise that I talk pretty easily about my trauma and my fight back. My family encouraged me to talk about it publicly and people seem to want to hear about it. So now I do a lot of public speaking - How I cope, where I find the strength and motivation to not give up and how I turned a negative, life changing trauma into a positive and ambitious future. If I can inspire anyone else to turn their life around, then my new life matters so much more than my previous one.

Finding Your Feet can get people back to sport and recreation; find hobbies and interests; get back to work; enjoy socialising and sharing experiences; providing support and encouragement to achieve the confidence to do it yourself. For some it's a life-saver and a life-changer, for others it's friendship or advice. It is inspiring and encouraging, and it makes me burst with pride to see so many people find their feet. Especially those who I didn't appreciate even needed to, like long-term amputees who hadn't been on a bike for 25 years, in a pool for 27 years, or who hadn't played sport through lack of confidence. And we laugh a lot together.

After three years we have movement therapy, a climbing club, abseiling, swimming classes, Ampu-TEAS (socials), ski lessons, a cycle club and day trips running regularly, as well as many one day specials like the cycle day, and the zip slide, and annuals like Christmas parties, Millport fundraiser, and the Arran challenge.

Another big success so far, though, was when Ashley was super-excited to be able to set up and roll out amputee football in Scotland. This gathered pace via the media and Partick Thistle FC coaches, and we found many new amputees who wanted to play.

We now have our original team in Glasgow, and the plan is to have several throughout Scotland, a Finding Your Feet league, and UK-wide tournaments. And, let me tell you, it's no lightweight game. A big guy running at you on two crutches is frightening enough, but you learn that they won't hold back for you so you have to get as tough as them. Our newly-qualified coach, Brian Murray, broke his collarbone at our first tournament when someone took him out. It's definitely not for softies!

***

Tracy Ralph, fellow amputee

The first time I heard Corinne's name mentioned to me, I was in my hospital bed in the Intensive Care Unit of St. Thomas's Hospital, London. It had been three or four weeks since I had fallen ill and been placed on ECMO, and a week or so after the amputations of both my legs and all my fingers. I still had my tracheotomy, so not only could I not walk, I couldn't talk either. Though my closest friends and family were strangely getting good at lip-reading.

The only people I wanted at my bedside were a select few family members and my three best friends — Karla, Nicola, and Natasha. The girls had found someone online who had been through a very similar experience to me just a year or so before — a lady called Corinne. They had watched a TED Talk and saw that she had set up a charity, Finding Your Feet, and had managed to obtain her mobile number. Nicola called her straight away, apparently not knowing what she was going to ask her but just to get some perspective, as my situation seemed so horrific for those living it every day with me. She tells me she spent the whole call in tears, and Corinne offered to fly down from Scotland to London to come to the ward to talk to them and to me.

For me, this was all too soon. I couldn't process what had happened to me, let alone talk to a stranger about it. I didn't want to see her. I didn't want to see anyone except those select few, but my best friends went ahead and arranged to meet her. Within a few days she had flown down from Glasgow to London City to chat with the girls.

I just lay in my bed thinking, 'What have you girls done? Why have you made the poor woman fly all this way down from Scotland? I'm still in intensive care?' I thought my friends were crazy; it just didn't make sense. I mouthed at them, 'Stop asking me to meet her.' But the girls said it had given them a lot of hope to meet her; hope that they passed on to me.

Corinne told them how she had managed to fly down on her own, walk from the airport to the tube, get on the tube and get to the airport — all with prosthetic legs and no hands. The girls said she was an inspiration.

I continued my rehab journey from hospital to Roehampton. When I finally came home in early June, I wasn't just faced with the mental rehabilitation but some upsetting issues which I had never dreamed would happen. Something clicked, and I knew it was the right time to contact Corinne. I wanted to ask questions, not only about my limbs and amputations, but also to speak to someone who somehow knew how I was feeling and how goddam hard all this was. I wanted to turn to someone distant yet someone who would understand.

I spoke to Corinne lots on the phone — she was only ever a phone call away, as clichéd as that sounds. In the November, she came down to my house with her son, Rory, and we had a lovely afternoon together with my best friends.

She quickly became a friend for life. She inspires me. I think she is an incredible woman, with a strength I can draw from. On my down days, she picks me back up. I feel like she's the strong one, and yet I wish I could do the same for her.

It takes something big in your life to make a change. And what happened to the pair of us was so unexpected and has had such a huge impact on our lives. When everything changes, you can go one way or the other; you can give up, or you can keep on fighting. And Corinne was amongst the people who helped me to fight. She has the same determination as me.

Now I have to go through another op, I'm terrified, but I see how determined she is and what she wants to achieve. I don't want to compete with her, but we are unique; we aren't your average Joes. And when I come out of the other side, after these further amputations, I know I can get through it. I want to help others; I want to help Corinne's charity, and fundraise for and with her.

I believe what's happened to me has happened for a reason, so that I can help people just like Corinne helped my friends and me.

I wish we lived closer. But a road to a friend's house is never too far... even on our legs.

***

Brian Murray, amputee footballer and Finding Your Feet Ambassador

I thought my dream of playing football was lost when I lost my left leg to cancer

when I was 10, but thanks to Everton amputees I started playing again 36 years later. Then, due to a taster session at Annan Athletic, we brought amputee football to Scotland.

This is where I met Corinne and Ashley, with the great charity Finding your Feet. And with the Partick Thistle Foundation, we have set up the first amputee football team in Scotland.

For me, this a dream come true and has helped me with my confidence in being seen without my artificial leg on. And my fitness has improved massively.

FYF have also helped me to take coaching lessons, which will help me progress others in the sport.

***

Maureen (Mo/Mor), bestie

I still find it hard to put into words how I felt when I thought I was going to lose my best friend. When her brother, Davy, phoned that first day to tell me it was time to come and say goodbye, it was almost more than I could bear.

Thankfully, due to dedicated medical professionals, and despite everything that has happened to her, I still have my wonderful crazy friend.

I am totally in awe of how she has dealt with everything, and think she is truly amazing.

Definition: Amazing – adjective

Causing great surprise or wonder; astonishing.

Synonyms: astounding, surprising, stunning, stagger-ing, stupefying, breathtaking, awe-inspiring, sensational, remarkable, spectacular, phenomenal, extraordinary, incredible, wonderful, marvellous.

***

Things I can't do:

I can't change my light bulbs as they are sunken in the light fitting, or those silly wee LED spots that are near impossible to able-handed people.

Earrings? Nightmare. Jewellery, in general, has been an issue. Elastic bracelets seemed a great idea but I've lost so many, given I have no hands to keep them on!

Gardening. I can't jump on a spade while holding it, and weeding is hard so I need to get help (hee hee!).

I couldn't open the doors of my Mini (I've now changed my car). Every other car is fine. It was a bad choice!

***

Things I struggle with:

I can't cut up my dinner, so I need to ask the restaurant or my companion to do it, like a two-year-old!

I buy pre-chopped vegetables. My bionic hand does it with some effort, but buying ready-prepared is easier!

I get lost inside my king-sized duvet when changing the bed linen!

Teaching Rory to do his shoe laces was a challenge. I can do my own with my legs off and using my teeth, but that wasn't a great way to demonstrate.

I have zip pull-uppers and button-hole gadgets, but I'd need a trolley bag to take all those gadgets with me every day, so I don't do my trouser top button, but just pull it closed with my belt. I'll pull up as much as possible, but it hurts to press so hard on a small zipper. Sometimes, I just expose myself and pull my top over!

For every little thing I can't do though, there are a hundred that I shouldn't be able to but I conquered them. There are many shortcuts that I have learned, gadgets that can help me and most of all a caring friend (or stranger) who is happy to help. Does that turn a 'can't do' into a 'I did it'?! There isn't much that defeats me though and anything that is really tough and frustrating, gets extra hours spent on it to prove that 'ACTUALLY, I CAN'

BEYOND BRAVE

A simple little cough was the beginning of her ordeal,
At first just ignored thinking time would heal.
She had no time to be ill, being a busy mum
Little did she know what was to come.

She had now begun her biggest fight,
Little knowing survival would need all her might.
Her life suddenly hanging in the balance,
with the odds very low,
Such remarkable courage she must now show.

A healthy young woman struck down in her prime.
Why had this happened, it was not her time?
Faced with the worst news that one could possibly hear,
Surrounded by her family and those she held dear.

An air ambulance summoned on a mercy flight,
Her family and friends with their fingers crossed tight,
Good fortune, technology and an ECMO machine,
Had saved the life of our dear Corinne.

Her survival, however, came at a terrible cost,
Her hands and feet she had now lost.
Her battle to survive she had certainly won,
Rebuilding her life had just begun.

Remarkable people like Corinne never lie down,
They don't mump and moan, or cry and frown.
They don't feel self-pity, or on the past do they dwell.

She is one of a kind that is easy to tell.
Her son, Rory, no doubt her greatest inspiration,
For the long road ahead on her rehabilitation.
To be the best mum for Rory is her ultimate aim,
Her outlook is fantastic; no-one does she blame.

A bionic mum of whom he can be proud,
She will always be there for him; this she has vowed.
Her football skills are improving, and she has such drive.
To be the best mum in the world she will always strive.

Her selflessness in adversity is an example to us all,
She now thinks of others despite her own fall.
'Finding Your Feet' was born with others in mind,
What a remarkable woman and so incredibly kind.

I was honoured to hear her speak
at the recent charity dinner,
The whole audience knew that she was a winner.
From the depths of despair to the stage at the hotel,
What is next for Corinne only time will tell.

The sky is the limit and she knows no boundary,
She is made of steel, straight from the foundry.
An inspiration to us all of what one can achieve,
The human spirit is amazing, I do now believe.

To Mum, Dad, Davy, Scott, and the rest of the crew,
Your Corinne is amazing, although this you all knew.
With her strength and yours,
together her life has been saved,
What a terrible time you all have braved.

With the many challenges Corinne has yet to face,
I know she will press on with a smile on her face.
Her charity grows stronger with the passing days,
To help others like her is what she now prays.

To think of others when her own world was black,
Is a measure of a lady that never looks back.
Her battles will continue and struggles she will endure,
She will never be beaten, of that I am sure.

With an insatiable appetite for life that will never diminish,
She is a woman on a mission that will never finish.
I wish her strength and happiness every step of the way.
From her mission I know she will never stray.

by Ally Anderson

THE LAST WORD (AS ALWAYS)
BIG BROTHER, DAVY

It seems so long ago that I sat with tears blinding me, typing out the initial '24hrs' blog. In the time it takes to say 'available only at your chemist', lives change forever. There is no going back, and the old 'me/ you' doesn't exist any more.

Direction has to be established quickly, and the momentum can only be permitted to be forwards. Today and tomorrow become the most important days, and yesterday ceases to be important at all. There are self-achievement goals that need to be set and rewards to be gained, and there are achievements we can bring about for others.

All of us know that the satisfaction gained from helping others far outweighs anything we can do for ourselves. In this age of social media, we all post Facebook messages and pictures to show others how much more interesting our lives are than theirs. The reality is that for most of us, life is mapped out and relatively mundane.

Sometimes it takes a life-changing trauma to show the world who we really are and what we are really capable of. Sometimes the worst thing we think could happen turns out to be the making of us. We become different; we can be rebuilt; we can become stronger, faster, better than we were before. Bionic.

Corinne is now a far more important person to the world than I am, or my brother is, or indeed than we are combined and doubled. She is 'The Real Life Bionic Woman'.

I look at her now and see a fully rounded woman that has found her perfection; confident, poised, and focused, and I couldn't be more proud of her. That said, she is still my wee sister and she can still be a colossal pain in the arse, but whatever happens from this point forwards, she matters. And mattering to the world is what we all have to aspire to.

If we all matter, we have a society and we are a collective. We all now understand that difference is just another shade of normal, and Finding Your Feet exists to embrace and highlight the '50 shades of normal' that lives within our society. I believe the world is richer for it.

There is an analogy that we use frequently about the relationship between the windscreen and the rear view mirror. There is a reason why these two pieces of glass are the relevant size they are, and it's to do with their importance to our direction of travel. We're all products of where we came from, but our growth — and in turn, our relevance to the world — comes from where we are heading. We glance behind but we focus forwards. We all matter; to what extent… depends on two pieces of glass.

Mel Gibson

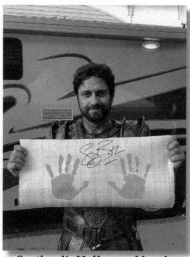

**Scotland's Hollywood hunk
Gerard Butler**

Robert Carlyle

Sir Andy Murray

Abseiling

An Officer and a Gentleman

Scotland's first amputee footballer

With Charlotte

Of course I can

With Tracy Ralph

It takes two to tandem

Bionic hand
© Caroline Stewart

Stay positive, stand tall
Courtesy of SALT magazine

With Davy, Scott & Cooper

Fun on two wheels

Rocky pose at FYF charity dinner

Michael O'Neill, Corinne & friends
© Drew Farrell